AN EARTH-COLORED SEA

General Editor: **Jacqueline Waldren**, *Institute of Social Anthropology, University of Oxford*

AN EARTH-COLORED SEA

*"Race," Culture, and the Politics of Identity in the
Postcolonial Portuguese-Speaking World*

Miguel Vale de Almeida

Berghahn Books
New York • Oxford

First published in 2004 by

Berghahn Books

www.berghahnbooks.com

© 2004 Miguel Vale de Almeida

Library of Congress Cataloging-in-Publication Data

Almeida, Miguel Vale de.
    [Mar da cor da terra. English]
    An earth-colored sea : "race," culture, and the politics of identity in the postcolonial
Portuguese-speaking world / Miguel Vale de Almeida.
        p. cm.
    Includes bibliographical references and index.
    ISBN 1-57181-607-0 (cl : alk. paper); ISBN 1-57181-608-9 (pbk : alk. paper)
    1. Portuguese--Foreign countries--History. 2. Ethnicity--Portuguese-speaking countries.
3. Blacks--Race identity--Brazil. 4. Portuguese--Trinidad and Tobago--Ethnic identity.
5. Pluralism (Social sciences) 6. Race awareness. 7. Group identity--East Timor. 8. Group
identity--Portugal. 9. Portuguese-speaking countries--Race relations. I. Title.

DP534.5.A46 2003
305.86'9--dc21   2003052193

British Library Cataloguing in Publication Data

A catalogue record for this book is available from
the British Library.

Printed in the United States on acid-free paper

ISBN 1-57181-607-0 hardback
ISBN 1-57181-608-9 paperback

To Paulo

CONTENTS

❧

FOREWORD AND ACKNOWLEDGEMENTS

This book is the English version—it is not simply a translation, since substantial parts have been altered—of a collection of essays on the politics of identity and cultural representation originally published in Portuguese (Vale de Almeida 2000). It analyzes the role of "culture" and "race" in the disputes centered on difference and inequality. The notions of ethnicity, "race," "culture," nation, colonialism, and postcolonialism are discussed in the light of ethnopolitical movements, anthropological theory, and official rhetoric on national identities. The structure of the book reflects a trajectory of research, starting with a case study in Trinidad, followed by another in Brazil, and ending with yet another in Portugal. The three case studies, written in the ethnographic genre, are intertwined with essays of a more theoretical nature. The nonmonographic, composite—or hybrid—nature of this work may be in itself an indication of the need for multisited, transnational, and historically grounded research when dealing with issues of representations of identity that were constructed during colonial times, and that are today reconfigured in the power-ridden struggles for cultural meanings.

*

In 1997–98 I did fieldwork in the city of Ilhéus, in the state of Bahia, Brazil. The research was focused on the emergence of the local "Black" movement, as the participants themselves call it. Since my 1996 book *The Hegemonic Male: Masculinity in a Portuguese Town* I had been redirecting my research interests from gender and sexuality toward ethnopolitics, "race," and the politics of identity and cultural representation. Before choosing Brazil as a field, I contemplated Trinidad and Tobago as a possible field for studying ethnic and "racial" complexity.

Chapter 1 narrates my brief experience in that Caribbean country. It is the story of a discontinued research project. However, it sets the tone for the book, since, while in Trinidad, my identity as a Portuguese placed me in a specific social position within the ethnic map of the country. Representations of the Portuguese immigrants in Trinidad highlight the ambiguous nature of the Portuguese diaspora in non-European lands: the colonizing nation was (and is) also a nation of immigrants.

An unexpected journey to Brazil triggered my intellectual curiosity and made me shift the field site from the Caribbean to this former Portuguese colony. Brazil is a challenge for a Portuguese anthropologist: it places him or her in an ambiguous position between estrangement and familiarity, because the language spoken is the same—and yet different—because there is a common history—and yet it is one of colonizers and colonized. Furthermore, the historical experience of the Afro-Brazilian population is, in a way, the outcome of Portuguese maritime expansion and colonialism, especially of its most negative side, slavery. Estrangement and familiarity thus give way to the need to reconsider the history of one's nation, its narratives, and their political consequences. The study of Afro-Brazilians' process of empowerment became also the study of the role of colonial experience and mythology in Portuguese representations of nationality.

Chapter 2 provides the ethnography of the Black movement in Ilhéus, Bahia, Brazil. "Black movement" is a local expression that designates both the cultural performances of poor Blacks (music, dance, Carnival, Afro-Brazilian religion, etc.) and their struggle for civil rights and social recognition (through different degrees of involvement in, and connection with, the political Black movement). This type of social movement falls under the category of ethnopolitics, that is, the mobilization of ethnicity (including "race") and "cultural products" for political purposes such as the recognition of cultural difference within the nation-state and the furthering of claims to the social and economic improvement of segments of the population that are oppressed by ethnocentric prejudice and/or socio-economic disenfranchisement. Although my initial intention was to write a book specifically about my research in Brazil, I eventually decided to include my materials in the form of a (longer) chapter in the Portuguese version of this book. In fact, the Brazilian experience set me on the track of studying the postcolonial reconfigurations of identity both in Portugal and her former colonies. This development away from the writing of a monographic work on the Afro-cultural movement in Brazil is further enhanced in the present English version: chapter 2 is now much shorter, in order to allow for an easier dialogue with the materials and discussions presented in other chapters of this book.

Chapter 3 analyzes the roots and ramifications of Luso-Tropicalism (i.e., Portuguese Tropicalism). As my knowledge of Brazilian history and anthropology deepened, I realized that the discourses on Brazilian national identity are intertwined with those on the Portuguese national identity. In particular, the so-called Luso-Tropicalist theories of Gilberto Freyre (1933) explained Brazil as a product of an alleged Portuguese capacity for miscegenation and adaptation.

These theories—which I classify as a type of "cultural exceptionalism"—coincide with those that, ever since the nineteenth century, have been upheld by Portuguese intellectuals and official rhetoric in order to justify the late colonial enterprise in Africa as the logical consequence of a national essence and purpose in history. Luso-Tropicalist theories have also become commonly held theories in both Portugal and Brazil, as well as among significant segments of the elites in other former colonies. This wishful-thinking narrative of miscegenation has been, of course, useless for the understanding of the conditions of the descendants of Africans in Brazil, the indigenous "Black" populations in the African former colonies, and African immigrants in Portugal today.

Chapter 4 further discusses the issues raised in chapter 3. Luso-Tropicalist notions deal with concepts such as hybridism, miscegenation and, although not in those exact words, in-betweenness (see Bhabha 1994) and creolization—all of which are the subjects of contemporary debates in postcolonial studies. These issues, however, have a long history of debate—both in academia and in politics —centered on the concepts of "race" and "culture." The object of that debate was, to a large extent, the colonial possessions, its populations and, reflexively, the colonizing nation-state and its peoples. This chapter confronts the paradoxical nature of the concept of hybridism by analyzing its history, particularly in the Portuguese colonial context.

Chapter 5 takes the reader from colonial times and extra-European locations to contemporary Portugal. The social movement of solidarity with East Timor that occurred in Lisbon in September 1999 demonstrated the importance to the Portuguese of emotional and cultural ties to people whom they saw as sharing their language and religion. These commonalities have a clear colonial history and are now being reconstructed around the idea of Lusophony (i.e., the commonwealth of Portuguese-speaking countries), which is taken to be the core of a Portuguese postcolonial identity. In East Timor, diacritical signs such as Portuguese and Catholicism were used in the nationalist struggle against Indonesia. These signs are the cultural patrimony of a local Creole elite and are exaggerated in Portuguese perceptions of East Timor. The colonial and postcolonial ironies of this case of mutual constitution of identity are analyzed.

Chapter 6 is a conclusion of sorts. It explores the relationship between the fields of anthropology and postcolonial studies. The latter is criticized for the lack of ethnographic grounding and for the historical and geographical limitations of its scope (namely, the English-speaking world). The "Portuguese case" (i.e., the social, political, economic, and cultural networks that were produced under the aegis of Portuguese colonialism) may establish a comparative field, provided that a new approach to Portuguese colonialism is implemented. Such an approach should focus on the anthropological aspects of the mutual constitution of colonizer and colonized identities, and this should be done within a critical framework that challenges commonsense Luso-Tropicalist approaches, by stressing cultural and historical specificity rather than cultural exceptionalism.

I could see the ocean from the balcony of my temporary home in Ilhéus and the beach was only a five-minute walk away. The tropical landscape and climate were in perfect harmony with Western fantasies of sensuous delight and idleness. However, I always paid attention to a small detail that seemed to soil this image of tropical bliss: the sea was unpleasantly brown, muddy, earth-colored. I have turned this fact into a symbol. The sea before me was the same sea that the Portuguese navigators had known five hundred years before when they "discovered" Brazil; it was the same sea that witnessed the arrival of slaves from Africa; the same sea that Afro-Brazilians symbolize as the road back to Africa; the same sea that is used as a symbol in the mythology of the Portuguese national narrative about maritime expansion. That sea is necessarily muddy, opaque, since it contains (and hides) multiple sediments, histories, and meanings, power and powerlessness, nostalgia for the past, and promises of liberation.

*

The writing of this book and the research it is based on would not have been possible without the help of many people. In Trinidad, Jo-Anne Ferreira was my main collaborator, but also my guide to sources and bibliography and, ultimately, a close friend.

In Ilhéus, I am indebted to the Rodrigues family from the neighborhood of Conquista, the Tombency religious *terreiro* and the Dilazenze Carnival *Bloco*. I shall always remember Mãe Hilsa, Marinho, Gleyde, Ney, and Dino as the best and most welcoming of field collaborators. Moacir Pinho, at the Ilhéus' Foundation for Cultural Activities, introduced me to the activists in the Black movement and the local politicians. All the members of the Council of Black Entities of Ilhéus were extremely open and helpful, namely Mãezinha, Val, Franklin, Sílvio, Jaco, Gurita, and Mãe Gessy; Gerson, although not a member of the council, provided me with useful information on the local "racial" politics regarding Carnival celebrations.

At the local university (Universidade Estadual de Santa Cruz), I am indebted to Professor Ruy Póvoas and the people at Kawe (Afro-Brazilian research group), *Capoeira* instructor Roberto, and dance instructor Lurdes. A special thanks is due to Jane Badaró Voisin, professor of Portuguese literature, who became one of my dearest friends: I was always welcomed at her home in Itacaré and miss the company of her husband, Pascal, and her children, Rafa and Joana.

In Olivença, the suburb of Ilhéus where I lived, life would not have been the same without the company and help of our neighbors the Magalhães: Cláudio, Élvio, Élvia, Isabel—and also *Mestre* Ramiro. The same applies to *Dona* Jó's food, her adopted child Carmen's smile and curiosity, and Elma's housekeeping. In Canavieiras, I enjoyed short vacations at the home of Miguel Mateus and Eveline Brigham, and in Salvador, life became more exciting at Bruno Visco's.

During fieldwork, my colleague Ana Cláudia Cruz da Silva shared information, data, and research tips without the hassles of competition, and her supervisor, Márcio Goldman (from the Federal University of Rio de Janeiro and a long time researcher of Ilhéus Afro-Brazilian community) has provided important insights for my work. At the University of Brasilia, Professors Alcida Ramos and Mariza Peirano showed a genuine interest in my work, inviting me to give a lecture on the work in progress. Journeys to Salvador were intellectually stimulating in the company of Pedro Agostinho and Maria do Rosário Carvalho (from the Federal University of Bahia); the same should be said of Cecilia McCallum's welcoming in Valença and, later on, at a conference she organized in Salvador.

My stay on the field in Brazil was shared with my colleague Susana de Matos Viegas, who was doing research with the local descendants of Indians. We shared a home, everyday life, troubles and hopes, and continue now to share both ideas and friendship. The frequent guests made the field feel more like home: for that I thank my parents; my old friend Rui Zink; Ruy Duarte de Carvalho; Pedro, Mónica, and Catarina; Leonor and Maria; Nuno Porto; and Ângela Corrêa. Most of all, I thank António, who always had the patience and understanding to accept my absences on the field.

Research in Brazil was funded by the Fundação para a Ciência e Tecnologia (Portuguese Ministry of Science). Administration tasks were carried out by Catarina Mira, at the Centro de Estudos de Antropologia Social (Instituto Superior de Ciências do Trabalho e da Empresa), which was the host institution for the research project. Celta Editora published the Portuguese version of my work, thanks to the enthusiasm of Rui Pena Pires. It should also be noted that some of this book's materials have already been published in academic journals (mostly in Portugal and Brazil) and due credit is given in each of the relevant chapters. Substantial parts of this book have been discussed in several seminars and conferences, to whose organizers I am grateful: Bela Feldman-Bianco, Mariza Corrêa, Cristiana Bastos, João Leal, Boaventura de Sousa Santos, Rosa Maria Perez, Clara Carvalho, Andrea Klimt, and Stephen Lubkemann. João de Pina Cabral has taken part in most of those events and has consistently contributed with constructive criticism of my work. I am also grateful to Margarida Lima de Faria at IICT (Institute for Tropical Research, Ministry of Science), Lisbon, for allowing time and space to write this book amidst my tasks at the Institute.

Finally, I dedicate this book to Paulo. I decided to write this version in English when I was visiting him in Cambridge, Massachusetts. It was there, too (on a subsequent visit) that I started writing. The book was finished in our new home in Lisbon. My decision to work on this project owes a great deal to the inspiration provided by his energy, friendship, love, and intelligence. That is only a small part of a much larger contribution: that of having turned my life into a much happier event.

1
POTOGEE:
BEING PORTUGUESE IN TRINIDAD

❧

"Is these Potogees who cause the trouble, you know," he said.
"They have their hands in the stinking salt-fish barrel and
they are still the first to talk of nigger this and coolie that."
(V. S. Naipaul, *The Middle Passage,* 1962)

In 1994 I visited Trinidad with the purpose of becoming familiar with what I thought would be a new fieldwork site.[1] I was interested in the Caribbean region because the local social formations were constituted by European expansion. Caribbean societies are products of the world economy of slavery and plantation, not a classical case of colonialism (once, of course, the indigenous population was exterminated in the early days of contact). Trinidad, in particular, is a society in which ethnic and racial diversity and modes of classification are complex and related to historical layers of forced immigration, indentured labor, and "voluntary" immigration. I had no intention whatsoever of studying the Portuguese of Trinidad. But my journey in that country was bound to surprise me: my acquaintance with a local Portuguese-Trinidadian scholar, and the subsequent decision to do fieldwork in Brazil instead, led me into writing this text. It is a text that tries to establish a dialogue between the genre of travel narrative on the one hand, and theoretical discussion on issues of ethnicity and "race" on the other.

Travel Journal

In spite of how small the island is, the ride from the airport to the bed-and-breakfast was long. The reason for that is that the taxi driver decided to stop at halfway. He did not tell me why he decided to stop by a cricket field where his fellow Mormon Church members were gathering for a picnic. I insisted on being taken to the bed-and-breakfast, since I desperately needed a shower to cool off the heat and humidity. But, for him, it would have been natural to stay a little longer. I was to find out later that he was not trying to proselytize, but rather simply performing Trinidadian "liming," that is, to let oneself linger, whether on a street corner, at home, or in a bar, just to talk for the sake of talking: exchanging information on other people's ethnic backgrounds; talking about a journey to Miami, Toronto, or London to visit relatives; trading tips on shopping and prices; discussing the merits of different songs in "soka" or steel band contests; analyzing cricket matches; or discussing politics. In sum, in liming you use time not in a "productive" manner, but rather in a "socially productive" way. You create ties and relationships, which also imply exerting social control, as it happens with "picong," a form of ironic sneering at other people's physical or behavioral attributes.

After two hours I finally arrived at Ms. Grace's. Her house is in Diego Martin, a suburb of the capital, Port of Spain. Grace is an elderly woman and a widow, she is active in the Anglican Church, and she asked me a lot about how to put her business on the Internet. My apartment was on the ground floor of her "Spanish-style" house, but I spent my first afternoon talking with her in her veranda covered with bougainvillea. I told her that I was in Trinidad just to get a sense of the place and to explore the possibility of doing research there. But my Portugueseness was to become the focus of her attention. She told me that I must meet the Portuguese of Trinidad. Having said this, she picked up the phone book and looked up Mr. De Nóbrega's (president of the Portuguese Club) phone number. She couldn't find it. Suddenly she remembered that a book about the Portuguese of Trinidad had just come out: "Let's call the author," she said. On that same day (and Trinidad has a population of over one million—it is not your tiny Caribbean island) I was on the phone with Jo-Anne Ferreira, author of *The Portuguese of Trinidad and Tobago: Portrait of an Ethnic Minority*. And on that same afternoon, Jo-Anne visited me, with her sister. Our conversation was quite formal at the beginning, maybe because I was perceived as much older—a side effect of precocious gray hair. She gave me a copy of her book. It was the beginning of a relationship with her, her family, and her friends. Let us take a look at her book, which I read in that same evening.

Portrait of an "Ethnic Minority"

People from diverse ethnic and national origins migrated to Trinidad as indentured laborers on sugar and cocoa plantations. The first to arrive were Portuguese from the island of Faial in the Azores, in 1834, the year of the abolition of slavery in the British Empire—a fact that generated considerable labor shortage in the plantations. The Azoreans' status was still illegal.

The first governmental attempts at solving the labor shortage crisis focused on Africans, Afro-Caribbeans, and freed slaves from the United States. The assumption was that they would adapt better: relations of production were racially essentialized through the use of the metaphor of adaptation to climate. Some local opinion makers, however, would rather have welcomed Europeans: "a stabilizing influence that would increase the number of whites in relation to Blacks and coloreds" (Brereton 1981: 98). They came from France, Germany, and England, but soon left Trinidad for the United States. In the aftermath of previous fluxes of Portuguese migrants to Guiana, the governments of Portugal and the United Kingdom signed a treaty on migration from Madeira Island to Trinidad. Contracts were to last for two years, and the first group of legal Madeiran indentured laborers arrived in Trinidad in 1846. Ferreira mentions economic and social crisis in Madeira as the main cause for migration: a crisis in the wine industry, the potato plague, a cholera outburst; apparently escape from compulsory draft was also a motivation. However, Ferreira also refers to a religious conflict. Thousands of Madeirans had converted to Presbyterianism in the 1840s in the wake of missionary work by the Scottish physician Robert Reid Kalley. Both the Catholic Church and the government persecuted them until the so-called Madeira Outrages broke out in August 1846.

The first group of migrants (219 people) arrived in May 1846, followed by 197 Protestants in September. Groups of 200, 160, and 216 more Protestants arrived in other ships throughout the same year. Catholics were mostly land laborers, whereas Protestants were more diversified professionally, since they had attended Kalley's schools in the towns of Machico, Santo António da Serra and São Roque.

If in the year of the abolition of slavery it was thought that European immigration could help "whiten" the local society, a few years later it was thought that significant numbers of European workers "would have upset the racial structure of society and undermined the dominance of the whites in the colony where Europeans owned and managed, while the colored races did the manual labor" (Brereton 1981: 99). The key word here is "workers": the will to "whiten" is weaker than the need to maintain a class structure based on "race." Soon the Madeirans were to be replaced by Indians and Chinese, but only after a second immigration wave, triggered by the 1870s phyloxera crisis in Madeira. By the end of the nineteenth century the Madeiran community had reached the figure of 2,000 souls. These people were not, however to renew their contracts: replaced on the plantations by East Indians, they either migrated elsewhere (namely the United States and Brazil) or became part of the local society as an intermediary social and ethnic group.

According to Ferreira, the Catholics opened rum shops and the Protestants grocery stores—a division supposedly based on different religious attitudes toward alcohol. The Protestants, however, would eventually invest in a strategy of international social upgrading: they migrated to the United States (where they established communities in Jacksonville and Springfield, both in Illinois) and to Brazil. Most of those who stayed behind were Catholics, and further groups of immigrants—this time free labor—were to arrive in the 1930s and also immediately after World War II.

The Portuguese were progressively assimilated at all levels: culturally, linguistically, and racially. In 1891 it was already said that "as with all other sections of the immigrant population, except the East Indian, the descendants of the natives of Portugal are being gradually absorbed in the native population" (Census of Trinidad and Tobago 1891, in Ferreira 1994: 23). Ferreira reasserts a common notion in her country: "No longer distinct as an ethnic group, largely because of dilution and assimilation through intermarriage with other ethnic groups, of both European and non-European origin, their descendants remain relatively few in numbers but great in influence and occupational status" (Ferreira 1994: 23).

Today's Portuguese community confronts Ferreira with a classic problem in ethnic and racial classifications in plural situations: after 1960 statistics ceased to define the Portuguese as an ethnic minority. Portuguese descendants were included in one of three categories: Europeans, Mixed, and Others. If in 1950 Smith identified 65 Madeiran-born Portuguese (1950: 65), Ferreira counted only 25 in 1994. She acknowledges the difficulty in identifying the Portuguese and uses the four categories set forth by Reis (1945): (A) Madeiran-born or Madeirans; (B) Creoles, the result of endogamous unions between second, third and fourth generation Madeirans; (C) mixed Creoles, the result of unions between one full-blooded Portuguese parent from (A) or (B) and a parent from a different extraction; (D) others, that is, people who have chosen to identify themselves as members of the community whether or not they are seen as such by members of (A), (B) or (C).

In the two ethnic associations, the Portuguese Club and the Portuguese Association, the main criterion for admission of people of mixed Portuguese descent was the sociological factor of interracial contact and mixture, "rather than purely ancestral or biological ties" (Reis 1945: 131, in Ferreira 1994). For instance, "non-Portuguese spouses of Portuguese members could become ordinary members of the Portuguese Club under certain restrictions, but not at the Associação Portuguesa" (Ferreira 1994: 25). Ferreira opts for a historical understanding of the ethnic group, as opposed to one based on self-identification. Thus,

> Those who "feel" or consider themselves Portuguese are generally those who still prepare one or more Portuguese dishes, those who take part in informal and formal Portuguese social functions and those whose families belong or have belonged to either one of the Portuguese social clubs or both. However, they may or may not agree that a community actually exists. (Ferreira 1994: 26)

In recent years there were some opportunities for the affirmation of Portuguese identity, such as the celebration of Portugal's National Day promoted by the Consul, the presentation of credentials by the Ambassador Duarte Vaz Pinto, and the 1989 celebration in the Portuguese community of Bishop John Mendes' appointment. These events seem to be promoted by Portuguese descendants who are already integrated in the "white" segment of society and who are therefore able to establish connections with both the diplomatic authorities and the official Portuguese discourse on "Portuguese communities." They become most active precisely when the Portuguese population is at its lowest, due to exogamy, aging, and out-migration. Ferreira stresses the fact that, originally, more men than women arrived from Madeira:

> One result of inter-racial marriages is the phenotypic immersion and absorption of the historical Portuguese community, so that it is difficult to ascertain those of Portuguese descent in the "mixed-blood" group, unless their surnames are Portuguese and unless they still maintain social links with others of Portuguese descent. (1994: 27)

The local representation of the Portuguese remained closely tied to grocery stores and rum shops. Until the Chinese replaced the Portuguese in the retail sector, stores were actually known as "Poteegee shops."[2] The social upgrading of the Portuguese—from small neighborhood stores to large scale distribution—is locally explained (as well as by Ferreira) as connected to the entrepreneurial and frugal nature of the Portuguese, their previous experience with retail trading, hard work, family ties, self-exploitation, and community solidarity. These "explanations" sound familiar: they are similar to those one can find in "national personality" studies in the Portuguese anthropology of the 1950s and 1960s, and they certainly should not be taken for granted. Ferreira, however, does not fully accept these stereotypes:

> An informant from South Trinidad remembers that in the 1940s, so many people in her village owed money to a particular shop owner that some of the village children would sing "pay Serrão, Serrão" (to the tune of "Que sera, sera"), so notorious a reputation was this shopkeeper's. (1994: 34)

Today there are no longer any "Poteegee shops," but instead large businesses carrying Portuguese names, such as J B Fernandes, the big rum producer. Ferreira uses the Portuguese idiom "nem carne nem peixe" (literally, neither meat nor fish) in order to locate the ambiguous space occupied by the Portuguese in the local multiethnic society:

> In a sense they bridged the gap between the European Creole elite at one end of the economic and social spectrum and the African and Indian proletariat at the other end. As Europeans, they shared the racial and physical characteristics of the "white" upper classes; as indentured laborers and shopkeepers, they occupied the lower strata made up of non-Europeans. (1994: 48)

Neither whites nor Blacks considered the Portuguese to be sociologically white. Until 1960 the Portuguese were included in a specific category in the census, corresponding to the "street culture" designation of "rash patash poteegees"—a deprecatory term that played with the sound of plurals in Portuguese. The local elite did not consider them white; at the most, they were seen as "Trinidad-white," and non-whites did not treat the Portuguese as their social superiors. Albert

Gomes[3] once said, in what recalls common notions about the Portuguese in Portugal itself, that "the Portuguese in Trinidad locked their color prejudices in their minds so that their loins might be unaffected by them. It is said that the Portuguese colonize in bed; certainly those in Trinidad were assimilated into the population in this way" (Gomes 1968: 9–10). The Portuguese were not able to assimilate with the whites until the period of economic progress triggered by oil drilling. This means that Gomes's and Reis's Luso-Tropicalism (see chapter 3) applies only to the relations between the Portuguese and the Blacks or colored. Jo-Anne Ferreira's book, nevertheless, could not do without a mention of one aspect to which all Portuguese descendants in Trinidad refer: the fact that ethnic identity in most families is reduced to certain eating habits. Among these, one dish is of symbolic importance—garlic pork (in English) or *carne de vinha de alhos* (in Portuguese). This is a Christmas meal, of Madeiran origin. Christmas in Trinidad (see Miller 1994) is a holiday in symmetrical position vis-à-vis Carnival. The former celebrates family solidarity and a feeling of permanence, whereas the latter celebrates ethnic mixing, volubility, and transience. Garlic pork is the key symbol for Portuguese creolized identity; it is an ethnic dish that is carefully cooked for that paramount moment of family commensality. The local name for *carne de vinha de alhos* is "carvinadage" or "calvinadage," names which resonate of "carnival" and "Calvinism"—but one should not infer etymology from a funny coincidence.

Travel Journal

A tacit agreement between Jo-Anne and myself was established: I would read and comment on her book (I would even help her translate one of her papers, to be published in a Madeiran journal), and she would show me her country. She would eventually introduce me to her family and friends and give me insights into the processes of ethnic and racial identification and differentiation.

Jo-Anne's family's home is a nice house in a middle-class suburb of Port of Spain called Petit Valley. She is a university student; she lives with her parents—both professional cadres—and brothers. Her father is of Portuguese extraction, but knows very little of the language. Her mother is of African ancestry: according to Portuguese categories of phenotypic classification she would be Black, but I was soon to find out the minute gradations that are used in Trinidad, where Jo-Anne's mother is considered "colored." The atmosphere in the house is welcoming and the conversation is relaxed and interesting. Jo-Anne's mother, a teacher, talks about the local racial structure in a very clear-minded and straightforward way. The Ferreiras don't see themselves as an exceptional mixed family. Their mixed condition, however, seems to dialogue mostly with their class position, their professional status, and their symbolic capital. It seems clear that the family cannot aspire to belong to the local white elite, just as it cannot aspire to belong to the class that owns economic power (which does not necessarily coincide with political power, since it has been in the hands of the Black urban civil servant sector for some decades, although it is being disputed by East Indians today).

Jo-Anne's family displays an antiracist discourse, which is not a mere question of political correctness. Their cultural capital allows them to have a historical and sociological perspective on what it is like to live in a society that was founded upon slavery and with a class system based on a racial one. They share a utopia of multiculturalism and multiracialism. But they are not naïve since they know that that utopia is part and parcel of the young nation-state.

Jo-Anne's family is an example of a segment of the population that is becoming increasingly important: an educated middle class, with transnational ties, and part of a global culture. This segment does not add up to a group, since all individual cases of such families were constituted on the basis of different ethnic encounters. Thus, ethnic and racial origin is hegemonic in Trinidad: it is the great model of reference for thinking and mapping out social identities. It is within it that changes of meaning and emancipatory projects occur, through semantic struggles. Jo-Anne was to engage in such a process: all the other members of the family are not as motivated for the rediscovery of Portuguese roots.

In the beginning I thought—rather naïvely—that Jo-Anne's research was an attempt at social upgrading in a context where ethnic origin is paramount. My train of thought was as follows: coming from a mixed family, the strengthening of her Portugueseness would take her closer to the "white" segment. But the fact that the Portuguese were considered as "neither white nor Black," especially because of their intermediary position in the economy, made me think again. I then thought that the recent promotion of Portugal to "Europe" could allow for a reformulation of the original idea. Furthermore, this happened when the Portuguese were no longer running rum shops and the community was disappearing. This could account for an identity that could be claimed by anyone who wanted to.

But why think like that? After all, the search for roots is not very different in the United States or Europe. Wasn't Jo-Anne simply anchoring her identity in a deeper family history, in a process that is common in modernity? Wasn't she, in a certain way, denying the logic of racial categorizations and strengthening the notions of "ethnicity" or "culture"? This was a complicated question, since the issue is all but a peaceful one in Trinidad, where skin color (and, indeed, tone), race, ethnic origin, and religion are at the core of conversations, disputes, alliances, and even of national politics and products of expressive culture, from music to Carnival. So that the reader will not get lost like I did while walking the streets—where a Hindu temple is next to a Mosque or an evangelical church, and Rastafarian motifs decorated the walls of a golf course for French Creoles—it is necessary to take a systematic look at ethnicity and race in Trinidad.

The Trinidadian Context

Yelvington's (1993) edited volume will be my guide for this section. In Trinidad, ethnicity is implied in the everyday struggles for power. For Yelvington, the history of Trinidad is the history of cleavages that cut across ethnic, class, cultural, national, religious, and sexual borders, adding up to a form of incomplete hegemony. This allowed for strategies of ascendancy that he coins as ethnic/class social structure (1993: 3).

After the extermination of Amerindian populations, Trinidad was a forsaken Spanish colony for three centuries. In response to the growing aggressiveness of the British Empire in the eighteenth century, Spain tried to make the island an economically viable colony, inviting French Catholic plantation owners from the Caribbean who were in a subaltern situation vis-à-vis their new British rulers. Thus began sugar plantation economy. Once the island was captured by the British in 1797 and formally granted to them in 1802, British planters also arrived from other islands, as well as groups of freed Black slaves (some from the United States, some freed from foreign ships by the Royal Navy, and yet others from other Caribbean islands). The geographical and linguistic origin of the Black population was from the beginning a very diverse one.

Three large socio-economic groups—corresponding to three ethnic groups—were soon established: the Whites, who were plantation owners or involved in business activities and the administration, controlled the resources; the colored occupied intermediary positions; and the large masses of Blacks, which included slaves, peasants, and agricultural workers. Ethnic rivalry was a fact within each group too. That was the case with the French Creoles (meaning French whites born in the Caribbean) and the British. The latter promoted Anglicization in a predominantly Catholic country with French culture as the reference (a Hispanic civilization was never established) (Yelvington 1993: 5).

With the end of slavery in 1834, labor from Madeira and China was sought after. These immigrants were to become the local small business class, later joined by the Syrian-Lebanese after World War II. The mass labor needed for pursuing the plantation economy was to be found in India: 144,000 indentured laborers arrived from Calcutta and Madras between 1845 and 1917. They were both Hindus and Muslims and were to resist creolization more than any other group. After their contracts were over, instead of returning to India, they became peasants.

Throughout the nineteenth century ethnic and occupational divisions were redefined: Whites remained as plantation owners, the Chinese and the Portuguese settled in commerce, the Blacks and colored ascended to professional trades, and the East Indians specialized in small- and average-scale agriculture in the rural areas of central and south Trinidad (in a regional opposition to the predominantly Black population in the northeastern towns) (Yelvington 1993: 7). Marriage between Black and Indian has ever since been a sort of implicit taboo; only recently has it gained some relevance and a new category—the "dougla"—was established for the products of those unions. Today the Black population accounts for 40 percent of the total population, but the East Indians have already reached that figure; it is these two groups that now compete for political power.

Yelvington's argument is that the process of ethnic identity formation involves "'sensing' likeness and differences and attaching meaning—and thus value—to those identities" (1993: 10). The initial resource for those identifications comes from above, from the groups holding power in slave society and particularly colonial power (see Mintz and Price 1976; Wolf 1982). This process has been referred to as commoditisation (Kopytoff 1986; see also Appadurai 1986): the formation of ethnic identity in Trinidad occurred in a situation of growing commodification of the labor force, a situation that was closely associated with a process of objectification of ethnicity (Yelvington 1993: 10).

These processes led to the commodification of ethnicity: subordinate groups were not only incapable of manipulating their own ethnic symbols, they were also not allowed to develop national images that would grant equal weight to all ethnic groups (Yelvington 1993: 11). This process affected Blacks the most. Not only were they the basis of slavery, they were also affected by a process of commodification of ethnicity at a global scale. Images generated and broadcast by the media, the international migration movements, and tourism provided the salient images of Blackness (Yelvington 1993: 11). I would add that this process leads not only to a global objectification of Blackness: as in the rest of the Caribbean, many Trinidadian families are transnational and import models of rebellion, too, namely from the United States.

The predominant notion that Trinidadian culture is syncretic—as seen in Carnival, steel bands, and calypso—is counterbalanced by the fact that political organization is ethnic-based. The two processes are not contradictory, as we shall see later. But let us summarize political events in the last decades. Universal suffrage was granted in 1946. Still under British rule (although with autonomy), Eric Williams and other urban Black intellectuals organized the People's National Movement (PNM) in 1955. PNM's nationalism, which replaced Gomes' government, wanted to erase ethnic differences and create a new nation. On the one hand, Trinidad was politically represented as a melting pot, but on the other, ethnicity penetrated PNM's ideology, since the symbols of the melting pot—steel bands, calypso, Carnival—were constructed as national symbols but interpreted as Afro-Trinidadian. Furthermore, Indians and their emerging political organizations opposed Williams's notion of "Afro-creolization."

The PNM remained in power until the emergence of the Black Power movement in the 1970s, already after full independence. It was a movement of working class urban Blacks who complained about local white and multinational domination of the economy. The movement forced the PNM to redistribute wealth in the aftermath of the 1970s oil boom. But the social changes generated by oil and redistributive policies did not amount to the submersion of ethnic identities. Rather, state patronage and clientelism grew. Mostly Blacks occupied political and administrative posts. This state of affairs has been strengthened in the last decades, together with a growing presence of urbanized Indians in the private sector. In 1986 the PNM was overthrown by the National Alliance for Reconstruction (NAR), a melting pot of class- and ethnic-based parties that was soon to break up along ethnic lines, leading the Indians to create their own political party. In 1990, Robinson and his cabinet were held hostage during an aborted coup attempt led by the Black Muslims.

Trinidadian society (like other Caribbean societies and some South American ones) has been explained by three different perspectives: first, by the theory of stratification, of a structural-functionalist nature, according to which society would keep its cohesion thanks to consensus around basic norms and values and in spite of diversity; second, by the theory of the plural society, which states that such a consensus does not exist, but rather that each cultural section keeps its own social institutions; and lastly, by the theory of the plantation society, which claims that social relations were molded by the plantation economy and that its social relations have not basically changed. Yelvington criticizes them all for not accounting for social change. I also think that they do not account for the role of the state, the insertion in global economy and culture, and the processes of manipulation, creation, and consumption of ethnic and racial symbols. However, one of the contributors to Yelvington's volume, Aisha Khan, uses a recent Trinidadian example, that of the construction of a "Spanish" identity (especially through Christmas "parang" music, sung in Spanish and originally from the northern mountains where the only Hispanic trace is toponomy). Khan, therefore, deals with mixed identities. Yelvington mentions her work thus:

> Rather than a discrete and bounded entity, "Spanish" identity is ambiguous and amorphous.... Khan traces the contingent meanings of "Spanish" to contexts of hierarchy and stratification, showing that why, when and how ethnicity is sensed, promulgated and contested is dependent on a wider network of relations of power. (Yelvington 1993: 19)

Although it introduces elements of ethnographic complexity whose clarification would go beyond the scope of this chapter, the following passage by Khan shows a good portrait of the semantic field of local processes of classification:

> … Various perceptions of possible criteria for "Spanish" identity: (a) "Spanish is white Negro mixed with Indian. It also has red Negro and Black Negro. White Negro is fair, clear, with straight or straightish hair" (Indo-Trinidadian woman). (b) "My daughter-in-law is a Spanish. She have an [East] Indian mother and a Spanish father, he is a red (very light-skinned Afro-Euro mix),[4] with kinda curly hair" (Indo-Trinidadian woman). (c) "We went through purely mulatto villages where the people were a baked copper color, much disfigured by disease. They had big light eyes and kinky red hair. My father described them as Spaniards" (V. S. Naipaul, *The Mimic Men*, 1985 (1967):

121). (d) "If I see the hair is straightish I will say Spanish, and if it is more curly I will say red … I look for skin color, hair, and what not. I say mixed if they seem more whitish, and Spanish or Spanishy if they seem more Negro" (Indo-Trinidadian woman). (Khan 1993: 196)

Note that Khan only refers to the perceptions of Indo-Trinidadian women. Throughout her paper, perceptions become much more complex, as the informants' social identities become more varied.

Although social scientific production is considerable in Trinidad and the Caribbean, one normally tends to approach ethnicity as a Western theoretical formulation. But Western theories tend to be excessively abstract and anchored in the society of the theory maker. An example of this is Anthony D. Smith's article in *The Companion Encyclopedia of Anthropology*. Smith's main concern seems to be with the nature of ethnic ties and sentiments (1994: 707). He draws a basic distinction between primordialist and circumstantialist perspectives. He introduces, however, a distinction between strong and weak primordialism. The former would be based on the universality of kinship and the latter in the perceived longevity of ethnic ties. Circumstantialist approaches, in turn, see ethnicity as a resource to be used for economic and political pursuits.

Smith connects this debate with a parallel one: that about the antiquity or modernity of nations and nationalism. Most authors seem to consider the nation and nationalism as modern phenomena, such as Anderson (1983) or Gellner (1973, 1983), for whom premodern societies were too stratified and divided to have a sense of homogeneity. Smith believes that both perennialists and modernists exaggerate the importance of the divide of modernity. He thinks there is an underlying fact that, in order to be understood, needs an approach to the role of symbols, myths, values and memories in the formation and maintenance of collective cultural identities (1994: 709), while accepting the importance of borders as studied by Barth (1969) and Armstrong (1982). When considering the factors that facilitated ethnic persistence, Smith emphasizes territorialization, war between states, organized religion, cultural isolation, and myths of ethnic election. The two main ways would be the Western one, of a civic and territorial inclination, and the ethnic and genealogical way (in Eastern Europe, Asia, and less so in Africa). He does acknowledge, however, other ways: the immigrant one (in America, Australia, and Argentina), and the colonial one—resulting in developmentalist nationalism (in the rest of Latin America and in sub-Saharan Africa).

Smith's perspective does not seem to be able to establish a theoretical consensus when one thinks about Trinidad or when issues of this general scope are brought down to acting subjectivity, as in the case of my friend Jo-Anne. One recent critical perspective on ethnicity becomes more important and useful in this case. But, first, the reader should be allowed to rest with a return to the travel journal.

Travel Journal

I interrupted my stay in Trinidad in order to spend a few days on the island of Tobago, thought to be Robinson Crusoe's island. It is actually, today, a territory increasingly alienated to German landowners and tourism operators, who arrive there on the nonstop flight from Frankfurt. I stayed at Mrs. Sardinha's, whose undeniable Blackness did not surprise me—considering her Portuguese name. I arrived at her bed-and-breakfast convinced that I could recover from a sleepless boat ride from the main island. But my hostess invited me to attend her nephew's first communion party. The social elite of Tobago was all there. Not that I understood it immediately—the guests were all very much at ease—but rather because I was introduced to Mr. Robinson, ex–Prime Minister of Trinidad and Tobago and ex–Black Muslim hostage. When I answered his question about what I intended to do in the country, I made the mistake of telling him that I would probably do my research in Trinidad, a more ethnically diversified island if compared with the very Afro-Caribbean Tobago. His reaction was compassionate at best: "You will never understand *that*. It's too confusing, too many identities. Stay here, it's easier. We're all Blacks here!" That was the ex–prime minister's answer, whose political enemies are mostly Indian. I was wondering whether he was right, while Mrs. Sardinha was enigmatically smiling at me.

Upon my return to Trinidad, Jo-Anne invited me for an outing. Together with her friend Shelley and her husband, we traveled to a remote village on the northern coast called Matelot ("sailor"). The idea was to have a picnic and to visit a Catholic nun who is one of Shelley's friend's aunts. I was already acquainted with these characters, descendants of Portuguese, Chinese, and Africans in several degrees of mixture, but all enthusiastic about discussing with me their Portugueseness and mine (I still don't know whether or not I was perceived as the real thing…). On our way to Matelot, we passed by Toco, where Herskovits did his comparative research on Trinidad and Africa. The countryside, the beach, the bathing in the river, the Creole food, all raised our spirits. On our way back to the capital, at dusk, Jo-Anne shot the question that was to start a lasting debate: "Do you believe in God?"

I shall spare the reader the contents of the debate. But it allowed me to know the story of Jo-Anne's religious options. Her sister and herself abandoned Catholicism a few years ago. They define themselves as "Christians," meaning that they estranged themselves from the institutional and ritual falsities of both Catholicism and Protestantism. From an outsider's point of view, Jo-Anne can be said to belong to an evangelical and Pentecostal group. It is an international organization whose main purpose is to translate the Bible into languages that do not have a version yet. She was asked to do her work in Africa, but she chose the Amazon forest instead, whereto she will be leaving shortly in order to do what we anthropologists call fieldwork. In her case, she will be learning a native language (as well as Portuguese); she will evangelize and, eventually, translate the Bible. It was "the work of a lifetime," as she defined it. At least as much work as it took to convince her parents, who only accepted Jo-Anne's choice thanks to their tolerant attitude on freedom of choice.

Jo-Anne's religious choice was the choice of a life course, a lifestyle, a set of values that she achieved in her church's communities in France and England, when she was there. Simultaneously, she pursues her Portuguese roots, and feels that she is a legitimate part of the construction of the Trinidadian nation as a multicultural society in which the main expressive cultural symbols are seen to be of African origin. In sum, things are a lot more complex than a matter of primordialism or circumstantialism, at least when we reach the level of specific, real people.

Ethnicity: Power and Differentiation

One can find a critique of current analysis of ethnicity in a volume edited by Wilmsen and McAllister (1996). According to the editors, if A. D. Smith's notion that ethnicity and race are versions of a human tendency to categorize and discriminate is not satisfactory, neither can one say that ethnicity is illegitimate because it is artificial (Wilmsen & McAllister 1996: 3). Wilmsen and McAllister shift the center of the argument to the fact that ethnicity emerges in the exercise of power (1996: 4). Therefore, several ethnicities must coexist in order for there to be ethnicity, and the dominant groups are never ethnicities, since they control the capacity to make hierarchical definitions. As stated by Comaroff in the same volume, ethnic awareness is a product of contradictions embodied in relations of structural inequality. Ethnic politics is a politics of marginality. Therefore, ethnicity is a relational concept. Although this does not seem to contradict Smith totally, it does specify that one is dealing with a relationship in which the dominant can define the subordinate. Dialectic arises when the subordinates adopt those terms by which they were defined as the basis for mobilization (Wilmsen & McAllister 1996: 5). The essence of ethnic existence lies on the access to resources and means of production, not only in the strict sense, but also in the sense of symbolic production.

Wilmsen acknowledges that ethnic terms work as condensers of traits—once independent—into one single symbol of generalized identity, "internal to the ideology of individuals who thus center a collective sense of selfhood" (Wilmsen & McAllister 1996: 5). Ethnicity and identity refer to "diametrically opposite processes of locating individuals within a social formation—the one to objective conditions of inequality within an arena of social power, the other to subjective classification on a stage of social practice" (Wilmsen & McAllister 1996: 6). Therefore, ethnic identity arises when and if those processes intersect. Wilmsen paraphrases Silverman (1976: 633), who said that ethnic consciousness and class "represent two entangled systems of stratification."

This seems to be clear when looking at the Trinidadian case. But, underlying both Smith's and Wilmsen and McAllister's perspectives, there is a questioning of "identity," a "concept" that does not seem to be very different from its use in common sense. In 1995 Rita Astuti presented a model of identity and difference that was meant to be an alternative to "ethnicity," while questioning also the current use of "identity." Based on the notion that "the Vezo are not a type of people"—in the ethnic sense used in anthropology—but rather "what they do and when they do it," Astuti suggests that identity is an activity and not an existential state. Identity is actualized in performance. A similar process to identification constructs difference. Thus, neither identity nor difference are inherent to people—they both are performative. This approach was meant as an alternative to those in which ethnicity has been seen as a form of primordial belonging or border maintenance, among others.

If traditional approaches have emphasized the notion of "shared origins," Linnekin and Poyer (1990)—one of the main sources for Astuti's work—claim alternative constructions of identity and difference. Both are seen as "ethnotheories." In contexts marked by colonization and slavery, such as Trinidad or Brazil, notions of race have been the classificatory resource par excellence. The idioms of class and color are used in a racialized fashion, thus naturalizing social inequalities. If to this we add the fact that in recent years one has been witnessing the creation of a taboo around the use of "race"—leading not to the overcoming of racism but to a displacement of the contents of "race" to expressions such as "ethnic groups" or "culture"—the available references for the constitution of collective, ethnic identities become more complex and fluid. This may lead to forms of cultural fundamentalism and strategies of exclusion, like those happening in European state policies and public opinion. In postcolonial contexts, strategies of exclusion led by socially dominant groups and by the states are confronted with, or mitigated by, strategies of self-definition based on notions of creolization.

An approach to ethnicity from the point of view of processes of power and differentiation does not mean, therefore, that one should blindly accept circumstantialist perspectives that simply accept the idea that groups opportunistically manipulate identities. It is the very notion of group identity that should be questioned, as well as the authority to establish definitions. These processes have become more complex due to global interdependence and the modern projects of personal choice of identities and lifestyles.

The Subjects and the World

There is a sentence in Daniel Miller's book on Trinidad that was crucial for my point of view while on the island: "From its inception Trinidad has been the creation of the global economy" (1994: 24). This means that the territory, the history, the sequence of generations that would have as an outcome today's Trinidad are the result of the process of European expansion, of slavery, of the plantation system, and of the construction of dependent peripheries by colonialism and, later, by multinational capitalism. I believe this context to be different from any of the regional ways outlined by Smith above.

According to Miller (and as we have already seen with Yelvington), no one group can claim to have achieved hegemonic domination. This has made it impossible to outline one historical trajectory that could account for a genealogy of modern Trinidad (Miller 1994: 22). In this sense, Trinidad is clearly a creolized society (and, in some aspects, a plural one) that continues to have to define itself in relation to other lands and its own origins. That is why the construction of a sense of being Trinidadian is done under extremely harsh conditions (when compared, for instance, with the taken-for-granted, although questionable, elements of being Portuguese in Portugal). Trinidad is a society with a strong sense of rupture, with a radicalization of the present, and without the reliance on a clear sense of custom and tradition (Miller 1994: 22). The strength of its identity lies, however, in the strong meanings of slavery, indentured labor, and colonialism.

There is no lack of origins in Trinidad, extra-Trinidad ones, that is. This leads to the feeling that today there is a simple pluralistic cacophony made of different voices and experiences, and this, to Miller, seems to fit the fashionable postmodern portrait (1994: 288). But, in spite of its creolized origins, Trinidad is not a cacophony. Miller's analysis of Christmas, for instance, reveals a highly normative ritual that creates a sense of specific and rooted national culture.

In another book, a volume organized by him, Miller (1995) uses the term "consumer" not in the sense of the free-choosing agent of economics, but as the opposite of the aesthetic ideal of the creative producer (1995: 1). His purpose is to reflect on contemporary conditions, in which very little of what we own is made by us: to be a consumer is to be aware that one lives through objects and images that were not created by us. This is what, for Miller, makes the term symptomatic of what Habermas (1987: 1–44) identified as the core meaning of "modernity" (Miller 1995: 2). Thus, the postmodern critique of superficiality attracted anthropologists because it opposes the ancient to the nouveau riche, especially when it becomes manifest among the lower classes of the West or among the Third World middle classes (Miller 1995: 3).

In the Caribbean, where families are spread out over many countries and where islands and states have been for a long time tied up to wider political-economic and social formations, it would be artificial to consider oneself as tied only to his or her "country" (Miller 1995: 12). But the pertinent question is: how specific is this situation of creolized, peripheral, and dependent contexts? Or: don't these attributions of specificity create a new exotic, opposed to supposedly solid identities in Europe?

Hannerz's (1992) contribution is among the most famous regarding processes of creolization in the contemporary context of globalization. Situations such as Trinidad and the Caribbean in general have always been ideal locations for the metaphor built upon linguistic Creoles, through any of the processes outlined by

Hannerz: acculturation studies in the 1930s, modernization theory in the 1960s, plural society models, or the theory of world systems. Hannerz proposes an analysis based on the root metaphor of creolization. Few people in Trinidad would oppose to it. Jo-Anne would not oppose it. Why then look for a Portuguese identity? I will try to answer this later in the paper.

Barber and Waterman (in Miller 1995) acknowledge the advantages of Hannerz's proposal, but call our attention to the dangers of bipolarization. Hannerz is, however, careful in marking these: the risk of seeing cultures as discrete units that mix in hierarchical fashion (Barber & Waterman 1995: 240). Note that in Trinidad, "Creole" specifically means a white person born outside Europe: he/she is the one who adapted to and was adopted by the local society, although he/she is also a creator of that society. Barber and Waterman reject the notion of hybridization because it might separate so-called indigenous from so-called imported aspects. They say that in the same way that cuisine transcends ingredients, so do other cultural expressions transcend their sources. It seems to me that in the Trinidadian case, however—because there is no "local preexisting culture" over which some colonial culture was imposed—hybridization exists from the beginning, that is, since the times of slavery, thus containing in itself the implicit power inequalities.

The problems raised by the concept of globalization are not all about borders and fluxes. Postcolonial thought, combined with post-structuralism, postmodernism and cultural studies, started a radical perspectivism focused on the culture/power nexus. The result has been the slogan of "multiculturalism," which is becoming increasingly problematic, especially when appropriated by right-wing thought. According to Joel Kahn, discourses on cultural alterity and multiculturalism are replacing the nineteenth-century idiom of civilization, temporal anteriority of the other, and the emancipation of beings as autonomous subjects (Kahn 1995: 15). We now see multiculturalism where we once saw a hierarchical diversity of peoples. But both visions share the logic denounced by Saïd (1978). Giving voice to others, as in postcolonial discourse, does not mean ending the separation between others and us.

When Homi Bhabha proposes a theory of cultural hybridization and of translation of social difference beyond the me/other and West/East polarizations, he is restating old anthropological questions. But he is not doing the same, since the talking subjects are people who share more with Jo-Anne Ferreira, for instance, than they do with a Western anthropologist. Bhabha (1994) analyzed the work of Trinidadian author V. S. Naipaul. He explores, among others, the concept of mimesis in order to understand the relation between colonizers and colonized. But it was in a passage from Naipaul's *The Middle Passage*, referring to 1914 in Trinidad, that I have found some illumination:

> Everyone was an individual, fighting for his place in the community. Yet there was no community. We were of various races, religions, sets and cliques; and we had somehow found ourselves on the same small island. Nothing bound us together except this

common residence. There was no nationalist feeling; indeed, it was only our Britishness, our belonging to the British Empire, which gave us any identity. So protests could only be individual, isolated, unheeded. (1962: 45)

Travel Journal

How much things have changed since Naipaul's memory of the early twentieth century … I recall, however, Jo-Anne's mother saying that that was exactly how she felt when she was young. She also said that independence had not taken away from her a sense of belonging to "something British." Most of all it did not take language away from her, or trips to London, or cosmopolitan references. But racial consciousness, she said, as well as the awareness of being in the Third World, in the periphery, became more and more important. She hoped that a more fair society would emerge, in both class and ethnic/racial terms. And today she feels that Trinidad is a project. According to Miller, what the Trinidadian ethnography suggests is that radically modern subjectivities can exist that are distinct from the autobiographical narrative with which Giddens (1994) characterizes implicitly Western subjects:

> Here individualism has to be constantly recreated at each event, in each relationship…its opposition to institutionalization is therefore continued through to a refusal to institutionalize the individual, even as biography. (Miller 1994: 309)

This could be the beginning of an answer to the previous question of why Jo-Anne was looking for a "Portuguese identity." This is probably what she has been telling me since we met. In the absence of national traditions and ethnic groups defined as the "true locals," many an anthropologist tends today to reify confusion and hybridism, or to highlight the creative potential of modern, *homo economicus*-like, individuals. But the Trinidadian case, and Jo-Anne's case, seem to indicate another path: understanding all contexts as contexts that are all (or once were) like the Trinidadian one, and characters such as my friend as potential versions of her. It reminds me of Marilyn Strathern's (1988) notion of the "dividual" instead of "individual" when she uses the Hagen ethnotheory to shed light on Western social theory: human beings have permeable borders and experience a constant movement between different aspects of social life. It seems a basic point, but it is often forgotten when we reify concepts such as ethnicity.

One year and many letters later, Jo-Anne and Shelley came to Lisbon. It was their first time in Portugal. They stayed for a few weeks, before leaving for Madeira where she was going to do some research on the local archives in order to complete her father's family genealogy. Portugal surprised her: she felt that she was neither in France nor England. But she did not feel that it was similar to "the other side," either. She thought that Trinidad was midway between center and periphery, but now the same applied to Portugal. She was also amazed at the way she was perceived in Lisbon, as a Portuguese emigrant visiting the home country. She was also surprised at the (apparent) suspension of racial categorization and confirmed what I had told her could happen: that she would "pass" for Portuguese, whatever that means. Especially if she said she was Portuguese.

We shall probably meet in Brazil. She will be explaining to the local Indians what it is to be a Christian. I will be studying issues that were the basis of my trip to Trinidad, but this time in Brazil. In a dream, there is a dialogue between us: "Why did you give up Trinidad as a field?" she asks. "Because I understood that I would find similar issues in Brazil"; "And so it is easier because of history and language, right?" I think for a minute and then say: "because I'm Portuguese. Or maybe Potogee." "And what is that?" she asks. And then she laughs.

Postscript

After having asked her permission to be mentioned in this paper, Jo-Anne sent me an e-mail whose content deserves to be known by the reader:

> … Actually for some reason I was musing on "(not) growing up Portuguese" in Trinidad just this morning. It struck me that I never felt "Portuguese," and never realized that I never felt Portuguese. So there was no vacuum, so to speak, since my identity was firstly based on being a Ferreira and Carter, a Trinbagonian (and later on, when I left the country, a West Indian to a lesser extent), and within the last 11 years, a Christian. But when I was in France, and Portuguese people asked if I was Portuguese, that had me wondering if it was a wild guess, or if indeed I bore any phenotypic resemblance to my Portuguese forebears (because I didn't where local Portuguese were concerned). Then later I read Alfred Mendes' and Albert Gomes' novels and saw Portuguese surnames in the context of Trinidad, and a chord was definitely struck, or plucked, whatever. And it was so nice to see "normal" names all over Portugal!
>
> Oddly enough, though we never grew up in the "Portuguese community" per se (that can be defined as those descended from (mid) twentieth century immigrants), not like us, from nineteenth century or extremely early twentieth century immigrants), all of my parents' friends were like them: each couple was made up of one Portuguese-descended (Trini) spouse and one not: a Corbie married a Gomes (female), a Cumming married a Gouveia (female), a de Silva married an Almondoz (female), and a de Silva married a de Silvia (female, from Antigua). Not to mention my paternal first cousins. Of Dad and his 13 siblings, 4 married Luso-Trinis (and produced 22 children), one married a Sino-Trini (3 children), 4 married "mixed" (including Mom, most of whom had Iberia in their family histories, total of 8 children), one married an Indo-Trini (no children), and 2 married other Euro (one Trini, one Canadian, total of 4 children). None (except one) of our generation went on to marry those from similar "ethnic" backgrounds (class and education are the factors now).

I suppose when I reached the age or stage of inquiry, which may have coincided with a general, national quest for ethnic identity in the country, and then I started to ask questions. I wrote a bit about that in an article for UWI [University of the West Indies], St Augustine's Oral and Pictorial Records Programme newsletter. I think Portugal was the first country (besides here) where I didn't feel physically different (culturally and linguistically of course, but I'm happy to learn like I did with French and France). Anyway, I rant and blab. Just thought I'd share that with you for what it is (or isn't) worth…

As the reader will certainly feel, this contribution was not only useful: it demonstrates how much the anthropological text can gain from relying on its informants' contribution. I am sure that Jo-Anne's reaction to this paper will surprise me further.

Post-postscript

And so it did. I have selected some passages from another and longer e-mail message in which she comments the final version of the paper that the reader is just finishing:

(1) … It was very interesting to note that you carefully redefined Mom as colored, according to our definitions. Her parents looked like me… (2) I don't think it is true to say that we cannot "aspire" to penetrate the ranks of the local white elite. The system here is not that rigid, and many races and mixtures are now part of them (except maybe the Arabs, who are another story). If we perceived them as something to aspire towards, we could if we wanted to, but we would have to change our whole value system and attitudes, and most of all professions and pastimes! (3) If I was trying, by my research, to infiltrate the local white group, well it sure backfired. Dad predicted I would make a few enemies or at least a few detractors, and so said, so done. The non-white Portuguese aren't really concerned, and the Portuguese and part-Portuguese whites aren't all thrilled. The more realistic and down-to-earth ones are. For those who are socially pretentious and snobbish and are trying to hide their past, well, I'm little more than a thorn in their sides! (4) Yes, my church is Pentecostal/Evangelical. But Wycliffe Bible Translators is an interdenominational and nondenominational para-church organization, and the Summer Institute of Linguistics is its academic sister organization. So they are not church organizations, although they are made up of church members. In France and England, I was at SIL, and in Brazil I will be working with SIL. Wycliffe in T&T sends me out. Do these precisions make sense? (5) … My intensely keen interest in things Portuguese stems from a love of family and love of country. Growing up, I knew more of my mother's extended family and much more of her family history, despite the ethnic, linguistic, socio-cultural and international diversity than I did of Dad's side. I was very puzzled that Dad could claim to be descended from one place and people and yet know nothing but garlic pork (which Mom prepares, thanks to Granny's recipe, and acquaintance with the dish before marriage through Luso-Trini neighbors). It was the constant and consistent lack of

forthcoming information (whether voluntarily given or reluctantly elicited) from Dad and his siblings (who really seemed to be strangely ignorant, like many of those descended from the nineteenth century immigrants) that provoked my natural insistent curiosity and prompted me to start digging. My digging was very personal before and was based simply on reconstructing my family "forests," and then naturally narrowed its focus (or expanded in some ways) to one ethnic group.... I didn't have a clue as to the research possibilities at the time. He [the publisher of Jo-Anne's book, who coached her into doing her research] asked me to go to the St Anne's Church of Scotland to find out about the Presbyterians, of whose existence I was totally ignorant. And when the Scottish reverend there actually gave me all of five articles, I was like "WOW—HOW interesting." Of course my interest was threefold: local history, Portuguese stuff and most of all, they were Christian refugees. So there was some measure of identification with them, although I am descended from the Catholics. (6) I love the word "portugalidade"! ["Portugueseness"—she is commenting on the Portuguese version of this paper] (7) I didn't know you thought we were being formal when we met you! That was very interesting, especially the part about the *cabelo branco* [gray hair].

Notes

1. A Portuguese version of this chapter was published in *Etnográfica*, I (1): 9–32, 1997, as "Ser Português na Trinidad: Etnicidade, Subjectividade e Poder."
2. V. S. Naipaul uses "potogee." During my stay in Trinidad, however, I was faced with this alternative spelling.
3. He was a writer and politician in the 1950s. He is the origin of the expression "gomesocracy," and he was the first to promote expressive forms to define Trinidadian identity: calypso, steel bands, Carnival.
4. Jo-Anne is often classified as such, but she refuses the classification on the basis of considering it the result of a local obsession with defining categories.

2
POWERS, PRODUCTS, AND PASSIONS: THE BLACK MOVEMENT IN A TOWN OF BAHIA, BRAZIL

> "That's everyone's problem today. How to love and respect
> what you are being taught to dissect"
> (Chaim Potok, *The Promise*)

Introduction

This chapter is based on fieldwork carried out between August 1997 and March 1998 in the city of Ilhéus, in the state of Bahia, Brazil.[1] The purpose of the chapter is to outline the strategies, the interests, and the appropriations of and by agents involved in the political and cultural representation of Afro-Brazilianness. These processes are seen as part of social tensions embodied in cultural meanings of differentiation and in structures of class and/or ethnic/"racial" inequality. Several intertwined institutions, groups, and activities were the focus of the research: the municipal Ilhéus' Foundation for Cultural Activities (FUNDACI), the Council of Black Entities of Ilhéus (CEAC), the *Blocos Afro*, *Candomblé terreiros*, and their respective neighborhood and kin networks, as well as body performances such as *Capoeira* and *Dança Afro*.[2]

The research also contemplated two other areas of ethnographic and theoretical relevance: on the one hand, the processes of definition of regional identity within the State of Bahia, mainly through local official projects of cultural and ecological tourism; on the other hand, larger-scale processes related to the Black movement in Bahia and Brazil, including the debate on race among social scientists studying Brazil.

This chapter is not, however, a summary of the research.[3] Its main purpose is to focus on a specific question: how do "Black entities" (as they are locally called) negotiate racial hegemony in the field of public cultural expression? The testimonies of three interviewees were chosen as illustrations of the process of mutual constitution of racial and political hegemony on the one hand, and the struggles over cultural representation on the other.

The Creation of a Local Afro-Brazilian Identity

Moacir Pinho[4] was in charge of all issues related to Black or Afro-Brazilian[5] culture at the FUNDACI. A concern with these issues was part of the political program of Mayor Jabes Ribeiro. The municipality of Ilhéus was in an awkward political situation: it was in the hands of a left-wing coalition, led by the Brazilian Social-Democratic Party (the same as Brazil's president), whereas the state of Bahia was controlled by the right-wing Liberal Front Party, which had almost complete hegemony thanks to the patron-client system set up by former governor and present senate leader in Brasilia, António Carlos Magalhães.[6] This situation weakened the municipality both politically and financially. The left-wing coalition needed constant negotiation of specific but antagonistic interests, including those of the Black movement and its different factions.

According to Moacir, the "ethnic" issue (he hesitated when using the expression[7]) was part of the cultural program of the local government, "considering the great expectations that were raised by the idea of having tourism as the main lever for economic development." His main concern was to define what is specific to the Ilhéus region, since "cultural tourism is today's most important innovation." In the beginning of the new administration, a set of cultural projects was included in a wider program called the "Zumbi Project".[8] These were "*Mata da Esperança*" (The Forest of Hope), "*Medicina Popular*" (Folk Medicine), "*Recontar a História*" (Retelling History), and "*Blocos Afro,*" as well as employment incentives for women and dance and percussion workshops for children in the poor suburbs. All the projects had a common assumption: that there was a coincidence between "minorities" and economically marginalized sectors, that is, Blacks, Indians, women, and the poor. The main goals of the above-mentioned projects were, respectively: to reserve a part of the remaining Atlantic forest for the exclusive use of the *Candomblé terreiro*s (mainly collection of magical and medicinal herbs and as the required venue for some rituals); to do a reconstitution of local history "from the point of view of the losers" (mainly by highlighting some characters and episodes related to Black and Indian resistance[9]); to salvage "Guarani" traditional handicrafts and language;[10] and to provide alternatives to the growing influence of commercial forms of dance and music.[11]

In the present narrative, Moacir Pinho represents the activist. He had recently arrived from the state capital, Salvador, and had brought with him political concerns related to socialism and the workers' movement, the Black civil rights movement and the Afro-Brazilian cultural renaissance. A member of the Workers' Party (*Partido dos Trabalhadores*, PT), he had come to Ilhéus as a consultant for the *Movimento Sindical de Trabalhadores Rurais* (Rural Workers' Trade Union). He started working for the FUNDACI in 1997. He was also the local leader of the *Movimento Negro Unificado* (Unified Black Movement, MNU), and was studying Philosophy at the local university (his area of study was the comparison between Afro-Brazilian religions on the one hand, and Christianity and Western rationality on the other). He was also initiated into *Candomblé*. One can say that his biography is exemplary of the connections between several institutions within the Brazilian Black movement, especially the roles played by the progressive sectors of the Catholic Church, by trade unionism, by the PT, by the post-1970s Black Movement, as well as by the processes of re-Africanization, especially the "return" to (and growth of) *Candomblé*. During fieldwork, his activity was focused on building a network of the local *Blocos Afro* and promoting their participation in Carnival.

Moacir Pinho's project regarding the *Blocos Afro* had two different names: first it was called *Ilhéus Caboclo*, then *Ilhéus Angola*. These denominations created a symbolic alliance between native Amerindians and Blacks. They also stressed the distinction between versions (or *nações,* i.e., nations) in *Candomblé* that only accept entities of African origin, from those (mainly Angola nation) that accept *caboclo* entities, that is, spirits of Indians as well as of other non-Africans. Although Moacir was initiated into Nagô *Candomblé* (an "orthodox," Africanist "nation"), he was confronted, in Ilhéus, with a strong Angola "nation" influence.[12] According to him, the "work on Black identity" had too many influences from Salvador:

> … The Black people in Salvador are not the same as the Black people in this region, from a cultural point of view. The presence and influence in Salvador is largely *Nagô*, Nigerians … whereas here it is *Angola*. The distinction is obvious in Candomblé. But in the so-called Black culture in general, the distinction is not so clear, because the institutions that publicize Black culture, mainly the Blocos Afro, work within a framework that is influenced by Salvador, they emulate Salvador. That is why we had the idea of starting some sort of work that local Blacks could identify with, because they are *Angola* Blacks. Now, this would necessarily create identification with the indigenous peoples. *Angola* Candomblé produced a sort of union with the indigenous peoples. In *Angola* Candomblé you can see both African *Orixás* and Indigenous *Caboclos*. People are receptive to this initiative, because ninety percent are *filhos-de-santo*[13] of *Angola* Candomblé *terreiros*. What I am doing is trying to call their attention to the fact that African descendants in Ilhéus do have this characteristic. This needs to be researched and implemented, so that the Black manifestations in Ilhéus cease to be a sub-product of what is done in Salvador. Even from an economic point of view, which is one of the main concerns of most groups and people in the communities. I have been telling them that in terms of local development, tourism can be a major resource for them. Tourists do not want to come to Ilhéus to see the same things that they can see in Salvador, where they are also more elaborate and structured. Tourists want to see something specific. And *Angola* is a specific thing. (Fieldwork interview)

Moacir's projects were not fully pursued. The only project that was actually implemented was the one regarding the *Blocos Afro*. The leaders of the Blocos were anxious to ensure financial conditions for participating in Carnival and pressed Moacir and the FUNDACI. The CEAC met several times during fieldwork in order to outline the contents of each Bloco's Carnival performance. That task involved choosing a theme, costumes, musical scores and songs. Establishing the amount of public funding and its distribution among Blocos was, however, the main task. Originally the CEAC encompassed seventeen groups: thirteen *Blocos Afro*, two *afoxés*, one *Capoeira* association, and one *Capoeira levada*.[14]

In order to prepare Carnival, FUNDACI organized a series of seminars on the so-called "self-sustainment" of the Afro groups as well as on artistic production and theme research. The seminars were ministered by the leaders of Olodum and Ilê Aiê, the two large *Blocos Afro* from Salvador, which are seen as the symbolic leaders of the Black political-cultural renaissance in Bahia.

Moacir wanted Carnival to focus on the "Angola" and "Caboclo" themes. He tried to guarantee this when he promoted the creation of a new *Bloco Afro*, the *Força Negra* (Black Strength). It was to be explicitly connected with the MNU and to inherit the musical instruments and the name of an old *Bloco* whose members had converted into an evangelical denomination.[15] Since the *Blocos* are unstructured organizations that are based on networks of neighborhood, *terreiro*, and kinship, conflicts around the distribution of funding are common. Three of the *Blocos* had ongoing and year-round activity, in contrast with all the remaining ones, which were mostly offshoots from the three main *Blocos*. These three—Dilazenze, Mini Congo, and Rastafari—were characterized by some favorable conditions: they all had some genealogical connection with the first *Bloco* to have existed in Ilhéus; they were sufficiently rooted in the local neighborhoods so as to have some self-sustaining capacity; they had more or less explicit connections with the communities formed by *Candomblé terreiros*; and their leaderships had stronger connections with the municipal power and/or were able to negotiate the support of political candidates who requested the services of the *Blocos* for shows during electoral campaigns. These characteristics allowed those *Blocos* to pursue year-round activity, not only during Carnival. The activity consisted mostly of shows and performances; this allowed for fund raising as well as for practicing songs and choreography. In Dilazenze's case, the activities also involved community work, the promotion of identity values, and action in the field of racial politics.

The first meetings of the CEAC were chaired by Moacir Pinho and took place at the FUNDACI offices. As the year progressed, the purpose of the meetings became the drafting of a charter and the election of a board. Marinho Rodrigues, leader of Dilazenze, was to be elected chair of CEAC,[16] at the same time that his *Bloco*'s dance group was being promoted through a show at the Municipal Theatre, as part of a series of shows by ballet and dance academies. The phenomenon of *Blocos* was, then, being rediscovered, since the new definition of "Cultural Carnival" was a priority in the tourism policy of the municipal authorities. That situation motivated all the leaders of the other *Blocos* in the CEAC to become members of the political MNU, since Moacir Pinho was both the movement's local representative and the person in charge of support to *Blocos* at the municipal FUNDACI.

It became clear during talks with Moacir Pinho and the leaders of the *Blocos* that the promotion of a specific cultural identity would be beneficial for all sectors of the regional society. Within Brazil—a country that has been globally commodified through essentialist labels[17] regarding music, rhythm, Carnival, multiracialism, and sensuous embodiment—Bahia is becoming the embodiment of a sort of Africanness outside Africa. In this context, Ilhéus wants to be defined as a Bahian subspecificity. This has traditionally been done through narratives that talk about the pioneering times of cocoa colonels, Jorge Amado's early novels, and icons of sexuality and miscegenation, such as Amado's character Gabriela. But these symbols are today seen as having an ambiguous relation with discourses on racial harmony. Black activists also see them as being too "white." The construction of a Black identity in Ilhéus is, thus, regional and segmentary: the latter has to negotiate the advantages it can offer to the former, if it is to be successful.[18] The tacit agreement among different sectors in society is restricted to the creation of performative cultural products based on the body and performing arts as well as on sensuous pleasure, which can be commodified together with natural beauty. Together they can target the type of tourist that craves cultural and natural difference. The cultural economy of this process attributes to Blacks the fabrication of these products. And it is precisely in this fabrication—this manufacture—that one can see the ambiguity between co-optation by hegemony and the potential for counter-hegemonic statements.

I shall try to articulate and confront Moacir Pinho's opinions with those of Marinho Rodrigues and Gerson Marques (former director of municipal tourism) so as to convey a notion of those ambiguous articulations. It is, however, necessary to contextualize their discourses and practices within a triangle of wider phenomena: the evolution of the Black rights' movement, the evolution of the politics of Afro-Brazilian cultural representation, and the evolution of interpretations of racial politics in Brazil.

The Brazilian Racial Formation

In a recent summary of studies of race and ethnicity, Bulmer and Solomos (1998) outline what to me is a strikingly accurate view of the issue. Following their analysis freely, the starting point for my consideration of the Ilhéus case is based on the following assumptions:

> Race and ethnicity are not natural categories … their boundaries are not fixed, nor is their membership … like nations, [they] are imagined communities … ideological

entities …, discursive formations, signaling a language through which differences are
accorded social significance … [with] material consequences for those who are
included within, or excluded from them (…). Race [is] a means of representing
difference such that contingent attributes, such as skin color, are transformed into
essential bases for identity. But this is not to deny that race remains, at the level of
everyday experience and social representation, a potent social and political category …
categories such as race and ethnicity are best conceived as social and political resources
… identities based on [them] are not simply imposed, since they are also often the
outcome of resistance and political struggle … it is more accurate to speak of a
racialized group rather than a racial group since race is a product of racism and not vice
versa … The terms of both official and popular discourses about race and racism are in
a constant state of flux … [and] subordinate groups may use difference to mystify, to
deny knowledge of themselves to the dominant groups … to stress their own
separateness, and to authorize their own representations … They may "seize the
category," claim it for their own and invert it, attaching positive value where before it
was negative. (Bulmer and Solomos 1998: 822–825)

Furthermore, since identities are not fixed, one has to pay attention to the fact
that essentialism may come from the subaltern field itself. The ambiguity between
multiculturalism and citizenship may come from this, because the politics that is
implied puts together equality and authenticity. This appropriation of Bulmer
and Solomos's ideas should be seen as my "itinerary" or map for navigation in this
terrain. Later I will add some "shortcuts" of my own.

The Brazilian case is particularly rich for understanding the passions, powers
and products associated with "race." It is outside the scope of this chapter to
attempt an all-encompassing study on the racial question in Brazil. A succinct
periodization and an identification of recurring issues are, however, necessary for
an understanding of the politics of culture and identity in Ilhéus.

The first period to consider encompasses Brazilian intellectual production
from the mid nineteenth century to the early decades of the twentieth century. At
the turn of the century the country was explained with a model that granted
"race" a primordial and foundational role (see Schwarcz 1993). European theories
of evolutionism and racial determinism were the main paradigm. A pessimistic
vision prevailed, one that blamed *mestiçagem* (see chapters 3 and 4) for the "racial
degeneration" of Brazilians. In the more radical versions, this vision claimed that
the young nation was unfeasible. However, the romantic "myth of the three races"
established an ambiguous discourse, somewhere between the reification of each of
the three races and the potential for their mixture. Although it was generally
conceived to be a factor of political and social instability, miscegenation was also
interpreted as a mark of national singularity and a possible future solution for the
racial problem. The ambiguities of miscegenation were to be "solved" by the
theories of whitening: Arian superiority would eventually guarantee the
disappearance of Blacks, Indians, and mulattos. Intellectual productions on the
issue of race were related not just to nation-state construction (as it was

happening in Europe, too), but also mostly to the issue of slavery and its abolition in 1888, on the eve of the establishment of the Republic and its social model inspired by positivism. Both the elites and the state attacked those manifestations of popular culture that could be seen as having an African origin, as in the case of the criminalization of *Capoeira* and the persecution of *Candomblé*. The justification was the fight against superstition and marginality among the popular urban masses, which were predominantly constituted by Blacks who had been marginalized from the workforce after abolition.

The second period coincided with the seminal[19] influence of Gilberto Freyre's *Casa-Grande e Senzala* (The Masters and the Slaves), published in 1933, and with the establishment of the *Estado Novo*, a para-Fascist regime. Freyre's interpretation of the formation of Brazil was based on the analysis of the domestic economy of the northeastern *engenho* or sugar plantation during the colonial period. He outlined the characteristics of Portuguese cultural plasticity: propensity toward miscegenation, mobility, and adaptation to the climate (see chapter 3). These would have led to a process of non-Europeanization of Brazil, a process that was supposedly achieved thanks to the role of Africans as cultural brokers or mediators. Freyre was widely accused of creating an idyllic image of colonial society based on a culturalist vision of Iberian familism and patriarchy; but his modernism, which was of a regionalist and conservative nature as opposed to São Paulo's urban, nationalist, and modernizing brand, was characterized by the desire to break away from the latent or explicit racism of most Brazilian discussion of the issue, whether on the "Brazil as an unfeasible country" version, or on the "whitening" version. Following his Boasian education, Freyre made a distinction between race and culture, and was to provide a version of national identity in which "the obsession with progress and reason … could somehow be replaced by an interpretation that focused on … the hybrid and unique articulation of traditions …" (Araújo 1994: 29). The *Estado Novo* regime popularized worldwide the idea of Brazil as a "racial democracy" in clear contrast to U.S. segregationism. Then began the phenomenon of appropriation by the national society of cultural manifestations of the descendants of Africans and slaves. They were co-opted as symbols of Brazilianness; nevertheless, they represented a specific area of cultural activity: mystical, bodily, musical, and sexual expressions.[20]

The third period—1950–1960—was marked by the UNESCO projects. The organization's antiracist agenda called for the analysis of the Brazilian "recipe" for "racial democracy." The Brazilian nonoppositional and gradative system of racial classification based on color raised curiosity and interest. According to Maggie (1993), the UNESCO research was initially designed for Bahia when Arthur Ramos—a Brazilian anthropologist—was the country's representative in the organization. The project, however, was ultimately extended to the whole of Brazil. On the one hand, it amounted to a comparison between the Brazilian model (based on phenotype or color) and the U.S. model (based on origin or blood). On the other hand, anthropologists did not cease to acknowledge and denounce social inequalities based on race (Nogueira 1955, Hutchinson 1952, and Harris 1970, later discussed by Degler 1971; the works of Wagley [1951] and Azevedo [1955] were also important at the time). According to Hanchard (1994), most of these studies were either charitable reexplanations of Freyre's thesis (for instance, Pierson 1942) or epiphenomenal treatments of race (Harris 1964). Maggie (1993), however, identifies a lineage of works that try to approximate models and social reality. She refers to DaMatta (1987) as a plausible continuation of that line. In his work he starts with the same model (origin vs. phenotype :: United States vs. Brazil), but rethinks both systems when he points to the relational character that presides over the Brazilian way of classifying Whites, Blacks, and Indians, in comparison with the American dual mode. Categories of classification used in Brazilian daily practice to refer people who are close to oneself—"from light(er) to dark(er)"—are extremely malleable and relative. In fact, there are few "Blacks" or "Whites" among one's close relations. They tend to be found only among distant third parties.

Different modes of classifying color were already obvious by that time: the romantic mode, based on the founding myth of the three races (Black, Indian, and White); the everyday mode (from lighter to darker); and the official statistical mode (*pretos, pardos, brancos,* and *amarelos*—blacks, browns, whites, and yellows).[21] The only mode missing then was polar classification (Black versus White), which was not to surface until Black activism in the late 1960s. The issue is clearly a political one and not simply a question of timeless and de-contextualized systems of classification.[22]

The fourth period, starting in the 1970s, was already subject to the influence of the transnational Black movements. Based on an analysis of the census, Hasenbalg and Valle e Silva (1988, 1993a, 1993b; Hasenbalg 1979, 1985, 1995) situated racial inequality at the center of economic relations as serving a necessary function in Brazilian capitalism. At the same time, they demonstrated that both marriage rules and principles of social upgrading are based on color difference, not on cultural difference (Maggie 1993). For Maggie, the so-called Black culture has not been the property of the descendants of Africans in Brazil. If the process of Brazilian racial hegemony was based on the cannibalization of African "roots" by the national whole, the space left for "color" as a classificatory resource has increased. Most processes of Black identity affirmation in recent years have been marked by the reiteration of a Black culture: they sway, paradoxically, between the affirmation of Black contributions to Brazil on the one hand, and a form of ethnicization that wants to free Black culture from the Brazilian melting pot (when it ceases to be seen as egalitarian) on the other. It is thus that "Black" ceases to refer to color, and starts referring to "identity."

What was the behavior of the Black community and movements alongside these scholarly productions? According to Agier and Carvalho (1994), three periods can be identified: the postabolition period that resulted in the prointegration movements of the 1930s, mainly in cities in the South; the antiracist movements of the 1970s; and the merging of diverse Black and Afro-Brazilian discourses and milieus in the period 1980–1990. Nineteenth-century Brazilian racialism established a clear distinction between Indians and Blacks: the former were granted the status of the ethnic "Other," albeit marginalized and excluded from citizenship. Blacks had supposedly been integrated through the official citizenship achieved after abolition, although they were kept in a socially inferior position. Today's situation is a product of this former construct: Black identity is affirmed through the production of a cultural difference of sorts (Agier & Carvalho 1994: 110), a process in which the Black movement finds itself face to face with the dilemma of having to deal with three contrasting identifications—*mestiçagem*, Brazilianness, and Blackness (Sousa 1997: 113).

The production of a discourse on difference has been centered on religion, on the growth and bureaucratization of *Candomblé terreiros*, and on the processes of Africanization of traditions (or, at least, in the attribution of explicitly African connotations to the expression "Afro-Brazilian"). The importance of cultural groups—started in the 1970s with the Bahian Carnival *Blocos*—is grounded on the inversion of negative and positive images. Agier and Carvalho (1994: 112) say that the main characteristic of these groups is the tendency to become official and lasting associations that counterbalance the instability of family institutions, promoting group solidarity and support. They become spaces for a type of cultural production (in music, dance, theater, poetry, iconography, and the aesthetics of dress and body), which is rich in African and Afro-Brazilian mythological references. Furthermore, this occurs in differentiated spaces of sociability in the city. In 1940 in Salvador the *Afoxé Filhos de Gandhi* was founded. It started undercover inside the stevedores' trade union, and later made its coming out as a group connected to *Candomblé*. The "*Blocos de Índio*" were born in the 1960s, a period of strong industrialization and urbanization. They originated within the samba schools, whose membership increasingly defined itself as Black, although in the parades they used the "mask" of Indianness, the symbol of true and original Brazil. In the 1970s, the *Blocos Afro* made explicit the connection between their "racial" identity and cultural Africanism. The renaissance of the political Black movement in the 1970–1980 decade denounced the existence of racism in the country, at the same time that the process of re-Africanization of some Black manifestations was starting. The year 1974 witnessed the foundation of the *Bloco Afro* Ilê Ayê in Salvador, later followed by Olodum and several others. In 1978 in São Paulo the MNU was founded: it proclaimed a Black identity under the notion of "resistance."

Although some important *Blocos* are, today, major enterprises specializing in the marketing and merchandising of Bahian Africanness, what characterizes them all is precisely the investment in cultural production and in the salvage of expressive cultural forms that were appropriated as national, all-Brazilian icons: dance, *Capoeira*, music, dress, food, and a religion based on performance and embodiment. Simultaneously these cultural products undergo a strong process of internationalization. Their growing popularity is also related to the growth of a Black middle class; the main symptom of this growth was the impact of *Raça Brasil* magazine (an avatar of the North American *Ebony*), targeted at an ethnically differentiated Black audience with higher income (in this magazine the traditional horoscope signs have been replaced by *Candomblé* Orixás).

African-American social scientist Michael Hanchard (1994) goes as far as pinpointing the "de-politicization" of race in Brazil. This is supposedly due to the prevalent commonsense notion of "racial democracy," to the reproduction of negative stereotypes about Black people and positive ones about Whites, and to preemptive sanctions imposed upon Blacks who challenge the patterns of asymmetry (under the rhetorical form of "if you raise the racial issue then you are being racist"). For Hanchard the main problem lies in the absence of two components of racial politics, namely power and culture. In the Brazilian racial economy Blacks are granted the role of specialists of expressive culture and sexuality. But the problem with culturalism, ever since Freyre defined Afro-Brazilian practices as an element of the national matrix, is that it leads to fetishization (a stronger expression than objectification) making it hard to establish the difference between culture as folklore and culture as the basis of values for ethic-political action (Hanchard 1994: 100). Hanchard does not deny, however, the mobilizing importance of the importation of non-Brazilian Black influences in the eighties; those influences helped create a kind of transnational identity among Afro-descendants, and are rooted in the early forms of pan-Africanism (and, according to Gilroy [1987, 1993], in the very transit throughout the Black Atlantic during slavery).

The historical process that created zones of contact and of mutual influence between intellectual production on race (in the social sciences), state policies, commonsense categories, and the cultural and political Black movements is, therefore, a complex one. The key points throughout this process—and which emerge today in the movement in Ilhéus—are the Brazilian racial hegemony, the culturalist inclination of the Black movement, and the tensions between the regional, national, and global levels in identity politics. *Mestiçagem*, whitening, and racial democracy are the three discursive knots in the Brazilian social formation and its politics of identity.

Carnival and the Struggles for Identity and Power

Carnival is the focal point for the activities of CEAC and the Black movement in Ilhéus. Carnival performances actualize the centrifugal and centripetal tendencies of racial and social segmentation. Gerson Marques was responsible for the municipal tourism authority for some years. When I interviewed him he had recently resigned from his post due to conflicting views on the model for local tourism development. In my narrative Gerson is representative of a social type, the professional cadre originating elsewhere (Rio de Janeiro) and knowledgeable of the national and global economy of tourism.

According to him, there were samba schools in Ilhéus until the 1980s. There were four of them, in the most popular quarters of town, which are also those with the highest percentage of Black population: Malhado, Conquista, Avenida Itabuna, and Oiteiro de São Sebastião. There were also some *Blocos de Arrasto* (groups of Carnival participants who, in the Venetian style, followed an improvised musical band) and, of course, the *Blocos Afro*. The first *Bloco Afro* was Axé Odara, whose successive victories in Carnival contests led it to become a band specializing in performing in hotels in the mass tourist resort of Porto Seguro.[23] Apparently samba schools disappeared because of the impact of the *Trio Eléctrico*, whose format can hardly be reconciled with traditional groups, because of the loud volume of the music, the large amount of space required for the huge trucks on top of which *Trio* bands perform, and the type of followers (see below). The *Trio Eléctrico* was originally a small pick-up truck where a band would play. Today they are heavy trucks adapted as huge sound systems. Bands called *Blocos de Trio* perform on the roofs of those trucks. In recent years these *trios* have been popularizing the so-called Axé Music, a commercial and pop version of Bahian rhythms that has been extremely successful. Some artists in this genre (Daniela Mercury, Banda Eva, Netinho) have gone international, especially in Portugal.

In 1984–1985, when the municipality was still in good financial shape, the organizers' task was to distribute resources among samba schools, *Blocos Afro* and *Blocos de Arrasto*. Gerson was in charge of that during Jabes Ribeiro's first six-year term of mayoral office. During the fourth or fifth year, the mayor tried to rationalize the allocation of funds: he established prizes and competitions. With the emergence of a financial crisis, Jabes was to be replaced by João Lírio, who continued his policies but was at the same time less enthusiastic about the cultural aspects of Carnival. Therefore, by the late 1980s samba schools and *Blocos de Arrasto* were no longer parading. The *Trio Eléctrico* was becoming increasingly popular and great show business names came to Ilhéus, hired by the municipal authorities. Conflicts between cultural groups and *Trio* supporters increased during Carnival planning meetings. The crucial change, however, was to happen during the administration of António Olímpio, the political adversary of Jabes Ribeiro. He supposedly took advantage of the renovation works in the Avenida Marginal to move Carnival to the neighborhood of Malhado; but he also anticipated the event in twenty-two days. This new Carnival on a new date became known as *Ilhéusfolia* and its main feature was the inclusion of *Blocos de Trio*. This situation went on for three years and Ilhéus's *Blocos de Trio* (there were three by then) "massacred the *Blocos Afro*."[24] The original idea of the *Carnaval Antecipado* (Anticipated Carnival) was Fernando Gomes's; he was the mayor of the neighboring municipality of Itabuna and wanted to build on the experience of Micaretas.[25] By anticipating Carnival in two weeks, Gomes was able to fight the competition of Salvador's Carnival.

When Jabes Ribeiro ran for mayor again, Gerson was in charge of tourism. He then devised two Carnivals: he wanted to keep the anticipated event, thus capitalizing on the growing success of Bahian music in Brazil, but he also wanted to restore the henceforth called "official" or "cultural" Carnival, provided that it would not include *Trios Eléctricos*. But the political situation (characterized by difficult relations with the State of Bahia and the near bankruptcy of the municipality) pressed for compromise in the debate around whether Anticipated Carnival was a Carnival "of the rich" or "of the poor." Three years had elapsed since the Afro entities had last paraded. On the first official Carnival of the *retomada* (the "renaissance"), in 1997, both Gerson Marques and Moacir Pinho pressed the mayor to subsidize the *Blocos Afro*, but they were confronted with accusations of conflict in fund distribution and of lack of quality in the *Blocos'* performances in the past (seen as too unprofessional and unspectacular).

The *Blocos de Trio* are emulations of the large Carnival *Blocos* of Salvador. They are entrepreneurial: a group of individuals invests the initial capital for making the costumes (the *abadás*) for the participants; these costumes are then sold and the profit is used to hire the bands that go out on the *Trios Eléctricos*. The "Galeras," or groups of supporters, are mainly composed of local people, mostly youths from the urban middle classes—at least that is the case with two large local *Blocos de Trio*, the Galera and the Borimbora. A more recent *Bloco*, the Eva, is the result of a joint venture between a local group and Salvador's Eva, which is a mega-*Bloco* with fourteen franchised offshoots throughout Brazil. It is a brand, and the tourist who belongs to an Eva in some other state may participate in Ilhéus' Eva if he or she happens to be vacationing in the area. Apart from the fact that *Blocos de Trio* concentrate on the Anticipated Carnival and the Afro ones do so in the Official/Cultural one, Ilhéus has been witnessing a growing representation of the *Blocos de Trio* as so-called *Blocos de Branco* (White folks' blocks). Economic inequality can thus be easily racialized, and vice versa.

In the meanwhile, the Anticipated Carnival of Ilhéus was privatized in the year of my stay. The streets where the parade takes place were closed off on the sides with boards, and entry points with ticket control were set up. Security was increased, and the ropes, which are put around the groups of followers, do not serve the function of protecting those inside, but rather keep away those who have not paid for their participation. For a Portuguese observer—but also for a Brazilian who might use the local system of phenotype classification—nothing could be more obvious than the fact that those inside the ropes were mainly White and middle class, whereas the security guards were Black.

Gerson would like an even more private space to be created within the event. He would like to have the parade happen in a sort of *sambódromo* (a sort of football stadium in Rio where the Carnival parade takes place). A tax would then be collected and the profit could revert for the support of *Blocos Afro*. For him, the main problem with the latter is lack of organization. Dilazenze, however, stands out as an example of how organization does not have to be entrepreneurial in order to be effective. One example of Dilazenze's qualities (which can also be found among Rastafari and Mini-Congo) is the fact that the *Bloco* was invited by Gerson to take part in an event of Ilhéus tourism promotion in a shopping center in Salvador. In most *Blocos Afro*, however, "voluntarism and the need to prepare Carnival fast as well as the absence of political and ideological preparation prevail: they have no idea how important they can be in this town." Gerson was referring to the fact that *Blocos* have an enormous potential to become institutions at the service of the integration of the poorer neighborhoods, in a context of a weak state and a weak civil society; and they are also strong vehicles for electoral mobilization. His complaint about the weakness of civil society is extensive to the white sectors, due to the specifics of the "cocoa civilization." Ever since the cocoa boom in the early twentieth century, local elites in Ilhéus became dependent on the monoculture and on the strategies of foreign-owned export businesses and fluctuations in the international market. They did not invest their profits, but rather spent them in sumptuary consumption, with no purpose of creating a local economic (and cultural) dynamic. Only recently did a new elite start to emerge, and Gerson includes himself in it, together with the mayor Jabes Ribeiro and his supporters, seen as the first regional ruling class whose origins are not rooted in the "cocoa economy."

His notion of "quality" tourism, as opposed to an imitation of Porto Seguro, resonates with Moacir's statements, although the patrimonial emphases are somewhat different:

> You have something to show, you have history. A pretty landscape is not enough. Do you have to have culture? Well, you've got it. Do you have to have history? We've got it. The forest with the highest biodiversity in the world? You've got it. Cultural tourism? Perfect profile: a place that is linked to the whole process of colonization and civilization of Brazil, which once was a *capitania hereditária* [an early colonial form of settlement], you have the whole world of cocoa production in Jorge Amado's novels, you have a history that the whole world knows as well as extremely rich cultural manifestations such as those that you are researching. This is Bahia and at the same time it has an identity of its own …[26](Fieldwork interview)

All local agents seem to agree: in this scenario, Dilazenze is the exception. It is the only *Bloco* that is able to carry on diverse types of activities throughout the year and the one that has the best performances in the Carnival parades. Behind the compliments, there is the acknowledgment that it is the most involved in the Black movement. It was born in the Conquista neighborhood and is led by Marinho Rodrigues. For the Carnival of 1998 the *Bloco* had prepared a meaningful theme: the history of the *Candomblé terreiro* from which it sprang, thus making that connection public and explicit.

Dilazenze

The carnal mother and mother-of-saint of Marinho is Hilsa Rodrigues, *Mãe* Hilsa (Mother Hilsa). She says that one of the most important moments in the history of the Éwé Tombency *terreiro* was the foundation of *Grupo Cultural Dilazenze*, on 22 February 1986. The proximity between the *terreiro* and Dilazenze goes beyond kinship. It is a fact that a great deal of the *Bloco* members are also adepts of Mãe Hilsa's *terreiro*, even her carnal sons and daughters, such as Mestre Ney, conductor of the *Bloco*'s percussion orchestra, or grandchildren, as is the case of Gleyde, choreographer of the Afro Dance Group of the *Bloco*. The relationship is even stronger than that, since the *fundamentos* of Dilazenze are joined with those of the *terreiro. Fundamentos* means the essences with sacred properties that guarantee the connection between the living and the ancestors in the lineage that founded the *terreiro*. One can say that they are the "mana" of the space of public ritual celebration. All the main elements of Dilazenze have to undergo *obrigações*, or contracts with the sacred, which cannot be undone for any reason. Unlike Catholic promises, which are payments in return for blessings received, *obrigações* are imposed upon people by the supernatural entities or deities, and must be followed in order to avoid unfortunate disgrace. Before Dilazenze leaves for the Carnival parade, Mãe Hilsa proceeds with a series of *obrigações*—of the propitiatory kind—which are offered to the supernatural entities that oversee the *Bloco*.

Marinho himself heads Dilazenze under the pressure of an *obrigação*, whose initial seven years of prescription have already been expanded for twenty-one years. It is obviously a heavy *obrigação*, symbolizing the importance of the *Bloco*'s work for the reproduction of the *terreiro* and the community it stands for. Since the *terreiro* has not had religious activity—in the strict sense of the word—for some years now (due to causes that cannot be explained in the context of this chapter), it is reasonable to say that the effort put into the *Bloco*'s activity may be a case of continuing action by other means.[27]

Dilazenze's activity in 1997–1998 featured two high points. First, they put on the first public performance of the Afro Dance Group in a space that is usually alien to these sorts of events—the Municipal Theater. The theater is one of two municipal infrastructures—the other being the Jorge Amado House—for the official representation of local culture. If, on the one hand, the house is an icon of the local origin of the famous Brazilian author (similarly to the Cocoa Museum, where the economic activity is turned into a regional cultural icon), the recently renovated theater indicates the desire to return to the era of prosperity and richness. Ilhéus has a proportionately high number of dance academies, catering to young middle- and upper-class, and mostly white, women and girls. The theater organized a series of shows to make their work public, and for the first time an Afro group was invited to take part in the series.[28] The choreographies are based on the reformulation of dance movements originating in *Candomblé* ritual.

34

The music is mostly taped African sounds, although some percussion rhythms from Dilazenze are included. The strategy of the Afro Dance Group is to confer cultural legitimacy on a certain kind of body line that is commonly seen as specifically Black but which, in the Cartesian dualist scheme, confers a subaltern status to its practitioners. In a similar way, *Capoeira* has been shown at the theater, but transformed into a sort of aestheticized and choreographed show that simultaneously confirms the interpretations of its origins in resistance to slavery, its Bahian specificity, and its Brazilianness.[29]

The second event was the seminar on Black culture, held at the Éwé Tombency *terreiro*. The stated purpose of the seminar was to analyze the experience of the *Blocos Afro*, Black presence in Ilhéus, Afro Dance, and the role of women in the Black movement, among other issues. There were very few participants in the seminar. Its meaning lies in the fact that the event reflected the *Bloco*'s and the *terreiro*'s attempt to build a discourse targeted at the wider community, using a language that would intervene and help build identity. Throughout the year, however, most energies were invested in the following: in assuring the working of CEAC, defining its charter, and electing a president (Marinho); in defining rules for participation in Carnival and for the distribution of funds among the *Blocos*; in helping define themes that would focus on regional Black identity and ensuring that the performances would have minimum quality; and in participating in public events that could promote the *Blocos* as legitimate representatives of a specifically regional culture. Besides this, a lot of energy was invested in doing shows at local hotels, in order to collect funds—with the collateral effect of thus actualizing the very specificity of regional and Bahian culture.

Dilazenze's performance at Carnival was undoubtedly superior in quality. The group had invited the "first lady" of Olodum as guest of honor and queen of the parade, thus symbolically receiving the legitimation from the "center," Salvador. The parade is composed of four wings: the dance group; the *Baianas*, who were invited from another *terreiro*; the small and rather improvised sound car (rented by the municipality and made available to each *Bloco* in turn), with the singers on the roof (Marinho among them) as well as the Carnival queen; and the followers behind, dressed with the *Bloco*'s *abadás*.

After Carnival, Marinho was complaining that the event lacked organization, and he regretted the fact that Gerson was no longer in charge. Marinho's complaints were targeted at the small group of people who conducted cultural policy in Ilhéus, a group that was involved with FUNDACI (thus inevitably including Moacir, who was in the embarrassing position of serving as intermediary between local municipal power and Black entities), and with the administrations of the Municipal Theatre and the Jorge Amado House. Those people were direct associates of the mayor, the most important being his wife, who holds the unofficial post of director of local cultural life. For instance, while commenting on the show in which Dilazenze participated in the Municipal Theater, Marinho said that:

… We wanted to reach out to a public made of tourists, not local people. The big mistake was that we believed in the partnership with FUNDACI, because Adriana [the mayor's wife] had assured us that there would be a good promotion of the event; but there was none. No such thing as TV or radio promos, sound car, posters, ads in travel agents, hotels and so on, like the Theatre does. Nothing was done. They didn't let us do the promotion in hotels ourselves. Because it was Dilazenze. At the same time there was a ballet festival going on, a festival with the academies which they do every year [*Dançando Ilhéus*]. All those academies were allowed to do their promotion. [Regarding tickets] they were afraid that once they would give us the tickets we would forget all about accounting for them, that we would keep the money, I don't know, they weren't believing in our work. That's when problems started in what regards the partnership. (Fieldwork interview)

There is a clear notion that Dilazenze felt that it wasn't trusted and that it was the victim of prejudice.[30] This is the sort of tension that prevails in the problematic relationship between Afro groups and the local government. Marinho's evaluation of Carnival clearly defines the guidelines for the creation of a local Black representation of identity. The issue that he pinpoints is related to the cultural and economic transformations of Carnival:

When the *Blocos de Trio* appeared, people from the periphery made sacrifices to go out on those *Blocos* and left the Afro ones. Now we want to take the debate into those communities, we really want a debate to start. I was talking with Moacir and he said "Man, Dila was the best *Bloco*, why is that?"… (Fieldwork interview)

The way to reverse those trends would be training in alternative cultural canons:

… I told him I believe that is because of the work we do all year round, people end up recovering their identities, their passion for the *Bloco*. We were always ahead of everybody: we held events in our headquarters, we held debates, dance workshops, all that started because our public today is young people, youngsters who don't know the first thing about *Blocos Afro*, so we have to prepare those people… They don't know anything about their culture. You have to work those people in order to value them as Black people, people from the periphery. (Fieldwork interview)

The definition of a Black identity is simultaneously a form of empowerment of the poor and marginalized sectors of society:

There are these girls who were in the dance workshop—they're from our street—and they will say, "if we take part in an event sponsored by Galera [a *Bloco de Trio*], man, it's gonna be great for us, to be among those people! Now, if we take part in an event sponsored by Dila or Rasta, all we'll have is poor low lives!" and so on. We want to give them their self-esteem back, we want them to dance the Afro dances, we want them to play, to value their culture. [He then emphasizes the work around workshops and seminars.] The more militants we have the stronger we are. But most people who are coming to us are already identifying, saying, "there's my real culture." But we still have to go deeper into that. We already have a project, we want to hold events all year round, with lectures, workshops and so on. (Fieldwork interview)

Certain traits of Black culture are seen as being more representative and in need of being salvaged because they are seen as ethnically specific, or as traits in need of being dewhitened:

> You see, people identified rapidly with the theme of our parade, with the *terreiro* theme. Some people took our guidelines for a script and ... [they recognized the lineage of Mãe Hilsa], it was as if their minds opened, they'd heard about it before, the identification was fast. We held several meetings with people from the community, we handed out the scripts. We did team work ... Ney would hand out the scripts to the percussion players. Some rhythms were made around that, for instance the Aguerê rhythm came up during those group sessions. And so did the choreography. Anything that would have to do with Tombency, with the Angola. Dances and *toques*, all was done with the theme in mind. People caught the gist of it real fast.[31] (Fieldwork interview)

It would not be excessive to say that Dilazenze is the example par excellence of the ambiguous dynamics of the politics of cultural representation of Black identity in Ilhéus: there is a history that is legitimized by the *terreiro*'s genealogies, which can be projected back into Africa, as well as in Bahia at large, and with a founding role in the region; the intimate relationship between *terreiro*, neighborhood community, *Bloco*, and family, thus providing a community alternative; the narrative and aesthetic definition of themes, music, and choreographies that define specificity, authenticity, and authorship; and the bargaining capacity—as well as difficulties—that are implied, considering a context marked by the trend to define cultural tourism as the salvation for the regional economy. The latter means that there is a tense relationship with the municipal authorities, with political and financial patronage, with the Black movement as a political movement, and with global trends toward the commodification of cultural differences.

Race, Ethnicity, and the Politics of Identity

This case of politics of cultural representation can be made richer if one uses the notion of cultural objectification in a dynamic way. According to Handler, it is a matter of seeing culture as a thing made out of objects and traits (1988: 14, and shared by Hayden 1996; Linnekin & Poyer 1990; Turner 1991). The "culture value" that underlies this representation and process may contribute to processes of emancipation as well as to processes of subordination. The definition of the "culture value"—probably an unexpected consequence of anthropological theory, like "race" was—is of a global nature, connected with the expansion of the market in cultural goods, with the modern romantic sensitivity made available by the industries that provide those goods, or with the fact that modern nation-states were not successful in providing all the materials for identity building and maintenance (Handler 1988). If culture is a "value," then, in conditions of global triumph of capitalism, the commodification of culture (which, as I see it, presupposes objectification) becomes obvious in, for instance, the promotion of tourism as the salvation for the regional economy. In conditions of social subordination—and this aspect cannot be overlooked in my case, because we are not in a multiethnic context made up of "equivalents," and there is a "racial" naturalization that is made self-evident in everyday life—the emancipatory potential for the Black segment will always be the most important aspect.

The process of emergence of the Black cultural discourse in Brazil contains a great deal of ethnicization. This happens, however, in global conditions in which the notion prevails that one has to belong to one of several equivalent differences. It also happens in the historical context of the political economy of the Black Atlantic (Gilroy 1993) in which there has always been a circulation—whether forced or voluntary—of people and ideas (e.g., pan-Africanism, *négritude*) that had to take into account three identity levels: the common African origin (implying a construction of "Africa"); the ethnic diversity of African origins; and the diversity of the colonial experiences, depending on different European powers. Most of all, however, the historical experience of slavery had to be taken into account.

Two problems permeate, therefore, the case that I have presented so far, making far more complex the issue of "culture value": they are "race" and its anchoring in political-economy and the body; and what in other contexts would be defined as ethnic mobilization. The naturalization of inequalities in Brazil (Guimarães 1995) was done with recourse to a racial use of color and class, contradicting on the one hand the idea of a nonracist Brazil, and, on the other, pushing antiracist movements in the direction of acknowledging race as a factor in Brazilian culture. They have to do it, however, in tension with habits of refusal of racial boundaries, grounded in the mystifying narrative of "racial democracy."

In this sense, the Brazilian case can be seen as an example of a dynamic of ethnicity in which body and naturalization play a determining role. As in any other case, ethnicity appears in the exercise of power, resulting from contradictions that are embodied in relations of structural inequality (Comaroff 1996). At the ethnic level we can witness attempts at circumventing those inequalities through solidarity based on a projected common origin or in attempts to perpetuate them—by means of naturalizing them.

We are used to seeing "ethnicity" in contexts in which the groups differentiate, through language or national/territorial origin, a consequence of the European romantic model of peoples and nation-states. One is usually reticent to apply the concept when referring to Afro-Americans in general, due to the intrusion of race as a naturalizing category, only because the context of the New World is not represented as having "different ethnic groups" within the same "race." Actually, the difference is not fundamental: the interpretations of the African origin or of the historical experience of the forced diaspora, slavery, and resistance, as well as the cultural production generated in that context, are enough for the emergence of a collective ethnic mobilization. The fact that this happens in a context in which there is a socially constructed perception and classification built upon an interpretation of the body may turn out to be a trap leading to reverse essentialism. But identity definitions are strategic and in order to be socially effective they have to give in to the cultural models of the day, not become paralyzed due to sociological skepticism, thus the emphasis on cultural forms based on the bodily arts by both dominant, defining powers, *and* subaltern social actors.

Using the Gramscian concept, Hanchard (1994) says that the Brazilian racial hegemony is articulated through processes of socialization that promote racial discrimination at the same time that they deny its existence. He says that he refers to "race" as the use of phenotypic differences as symbols of social distinction. Relations of power distribute meanings and practices that are then manifest in *asymmetrical* relations between groups, with race working as a channel between culture and social structure (Gilroy 1987). According to Hanchard, the problem in Brazil is how to build counterhegemonic values starting from the current ones without reproducing them under new forms; and how to fight for equality in the face of an ideology that says that there is no need to do so. The culturalist practices of the Black movement would be impeditive of the counterhegemonic political activities, because they reproduce the culturalist tendencies found in the ideology of racial democracy. Therefore, the depriving of resources, racial hegemony, and the culturalist inclination would be the main problems affecting the solidification of the Black movement in Brazil.

Hanchard stops where the anthropologist's work must start: in the way identities are redefined in political practice. That is what I have tried to demonstrate with my three characters, who are simultaneously individuals and representatives of different powers and knowledges. One cannot forget that people and groups who are marginalized by reasons of class, race, and so on, can enter a process of empowerment if they learn and sophisticate the Black or Afro-Brazilian cultural products and performances, to which they have *legitimate* claims (i.e. according to the rules of a system of classification based on a social reading of physical traits), thus defining themselves as Blacks. The Brazilian system is particularly good for that. It is particularly harsh, too, since those who find themselves at the far end of the dark-light spectrum may feel constrained to adopt Black or Afro-Brazilian culture.

It seems to be in the body and in corporality that the direction of the transit between race, ethnicity, cultural value and representation, and identity politics is defined, as well as the claims to common descent, or the valuing of body aptitudes. In the Afro-Brazilian case, the "culture value" mentioned above achieves a double complicity: it has to deal with the heritage of the notions of race; and its cultural capital is made up of cultural products anchored in

39

embodiment and corporality. But polar inversion apart (negative attributes into positive), whatever happened to the old anthropological separation between race and culture, when in many European contexts culture (and ethnic group) takes the place left empty by the damnation of race and, in contexts such as Brazil, race seems now to take the place once conquered by culture?

This is a question for the future. But in Ilhéus the historical legacy of the double marginalization by class and race and the juxtaposition between classification system and social hierarchy became evident. Empowerment is achieved in the delicate negotiation of given meanings and redefined meanings. The moment is strained and dense precisely because once the idiom of culture has become universally valued, the easiest strategy is that of culturalism, which unfolds, on the one hand, as commodification and cultural objectification and, on the other, as its embodiment. There it comes too dangerously close to the fire of race. But my informants did not light that fire. During my stay with them I learned that one can only work with the tools one has. When I went out with Dilazenze during Carnival, I *understood* the enormous passion and power that music and dance broadcast. For a moment I reversed the "Black skin/white mask" duality of Fanon (1952). But I shall *never understand* what it is like to have in one's body the socially defined mark of subalternity.

Passions lived, powers imposed and claimed, products created—none were rhetorical amusements, but rather sensed and felt subalternities.

Notes

1. A similar version of this chapter was published as an article, in Portuguese: "Poderes, Produtos, Paixões: O Movimento Negro numa Cidade Baiana," *Etnográfica* 3 (1): 131–156, 1999.
2. A *Bloco Afro* is an association or club that takes part in the annual Carnival parade. It consists of a band, a dance group, and the followers. *Candomblé* is an Afro-Brazilian religion, based on the cult of the ancestors and spirits, through incorporation during trance. A *terreiro* is a *Candomblé* congregation, led by a *mãe-de-santo* or *pai-de-santo*. *Capoeira* is a martial art or sport of alleged African origin. *Dança Afro* is the designation for dance forms that are inspired in *Candomblé* ritual dancing.
3. The Portuguese version of this book includes a much longer chapter, with the full ethnographic account of my Brazilian research. See Vale de Almeida (2000).
4. The names are real. Fieldwork was conducted without any hidden agenda. It focused on public policy issues, and my interviewees were fully informed on the nature and purpose of my research.
5. The use of either expression corresponds to different attitudes and values in different political contexts, as will become clear throughout the chapter.
6. The political patron-client system in Bahia can be seen as the continuation by other means of the institution of *coronelismo*, a form of electoral patron-client relations that was supported by networks of economic dependence during the period of land takeover for cocoa plantations in the late nineteenth and early twentieth centuries. Landowners with political influence were called "coronels" because they were honorary members of the National Guard.
7. The hesitation may have to do with the fact that the Brazilian commonsense meaning for "ethnic group" relates mainly to indigenous or immigrant groups. The ascription of Afro-

Brazilians to the category "race" is a problem for the Black movement activists, since the category "ethnic" could give them the chance of inclusion in a logic of multicultural difference, therefore avoiding racialism. "Race," however, allows them to establish transhistorical and transnational connections with the whole of the "Black Atlantic"; it also grants Blacks a foundational role within the national representations of the "three-race Brazil" (as explained later in the chapter).

8. Zumbi was the leader of the *quilombo* (community of runaway slaves) of Palmares during the colonial period. The Black movement has recovered him as the personification of resistance against slavery. In the last decade he has been included, by the Brazilian state, in the pantheon of national heroes.

9. There are three such episodes: the "battle of the *navegadores* (sailors)" or "*nadadores*" (swimmers), which opposed settlers and indigenous populations during the pioneer period; *caboclo* (mixed Indian and White, but also generic name for Indian) Marcelino, who was chased by cocoa planters and the authorities because of his calls for social (and ethnic?) revolt; and the rebellion at the Engenho (plantation) de Santana, interpreted today as the first strike conducted by slaves who were inspired by news of the French and Haitian revolutions. The anthropological relevance of these episodes lies in the frailty of historical certainty and in the richness of mythical interpretations that it allows for.

10. My colleague Susana Viegas focused her research on the local *caboclo* populations. The ethnic denomination "Guarani" for the descendants of Indians is totally spurious. See Viegas (1998).

11. Moacir Pinho was referring to the *tchan*, the *dança da bundinha*, and other commercial choreographies that exploit commonsense notions on the supposed sensuality and bodily attributes of Blacks, specifically Black women.

12. It was the nineteenth-century physician and anthropologist Nina Rodrigues who conferred authority to the distinction between "nations," seen as the continuation in Brazil of different African ethnic groups. For *Candomblé* believers, "nations" define different rites, specifications of language and idiom, musical rhythms, patterns of dancing, and the pantheon of spiritual and divine entities. But all nations dialogue with each other and the borders are not too rigid, except among the recent orthodox minorities who ascribe to Africanization according to a Yoruba model. On Nina Rodrigues and the first racialist systematic in Brazil, see Corrêa (1998).

13. People who have been initiated in *Candomblé* religion.

14. An *afoxé* is a group of *Candomblé* initiates that goes out on Carnival in order to show dances that originate in the *terreiro*; a *levada da capoeira* is a group of *Capoeira* fighters that take to the streets in the Carnival parade.

15. Evangelism, especially the neo-Pentecostal denominations, is seen by both Black movement leaders and by *pais-de-santo* and *mães-de-santo* as the greatest threat to Afro-Brazilian religion since the time when it was banned, because recruitment is made among the same population. In the case of the *Força Negra Bloco*, the converted members became a musical band that won evangelical music awards. The new *Força Negra* tried to use the *terreiro* led by the *mãe-de-santo* (also carnal mother) of one of its members as headquarters and basis for recruitment. But the *Bloco*, which was started from the top down, was not successful and did not even present itself during the 1998 Carnival.

16. It is important to note that nothing in this process should be seen as a well-organized movement. Meetings were often postponed or lacked a quorum, the agendas were not always explicit, and the progress in decision making was always slow. There was a great lack of knowledge and habit of associationism; this happened in a context in which democracy was recent and relations of clientelism had been established for long; the cultural and political capital of Blacks was extremely low. Furthermore, the movement was much more recent, weak and unstable in Ilhéus than in the larger metropolitan areas of Brazil. Both my colleague Susana Viegas and I, as well as Brazilian anthropologist Ana Cláudia Silva (who was conducting parallel research), helped in drafting the charter of CEAC and chaired the electoral assembly that elected CEAC's directorate.

17. As well as naturalizing power, since they are racialized (see Yanagisako & Delaney 1995).

41

18. There is a strong literary production in and about the region, not just Jorge Amado. Its promotion increased since a regional university was founded. But some Black sectors complain about the invisibility of Blacks within that literary production. Ruy Póvoas—a university professor who is also *pai-de-santo*—was promoting research on Black oral literature.

19. This is not an innocent image: Freyre's narrative is basically a narrative of sexuality and of the relations between desire and power in a doubly hierarchical context (in terms of mode of production and race).

20. The defense of the legitimacy and legality of African forms was also done by the Afro-Brazilian Congresses of 1934, in Recife, and 1937, in Salvador. Freyre was the head figure in the former, and Edison Carneiro in the latter. Both continued a process started by Nina Rodrigues: the definition of a sense of Black community based on the sociability of *candomblé*. This is a point that today's Black militants, who are influenced by a secular association between race and class, are starting to acknowledge—besides the fact that *candomblé* contributes for the construction of a Black Bahian and Brazilian specificity.

21. Census categories have been an object of dispute in recent years. The Black movement, especially the MNU, claims that Afro-descendants should be a category, including *morenos*, and *pardos*. Note that if *moreno* belongs to the idiom of color, *pardo* has historically encompassed the most diverse mixtures; it is a noncategory that common sense makes equivalent to "Brazilian."

22. The classificatory concerns of the UNESCO project were to be refined by Florestan Fernandes (1965), who established the nexus between class and race, thus instituting an approach that has many adepts today. His thesis is that racial inequalities and racism are both rooted in the system of slavery and in the fact that former slaves were not prepared for the free labor market after the abolition in 1888. But one must not forget that the period of slavery was also a period of resistance, adaptation, and mutual concessions between masters and slaves; social groups were more than two, including freed slaves, mulattos, mulattos who owned slaves, and so on (see Reis 1988; Reis & Silva 1989).

23. The fact that the place of the "discovery" of Brazil is today a mass tourist town is an irony of history that I cannot resist emphasizing.

24. The opposition between *Blocos de Trio* (which the more radical call *Blocos de Branco*—White blocks) and *Blocos Afro* is a recurrent theme. In the Carnival of 1998, Dilazenze had a skirmish with a *trio* that was going in the opposite direction in the parade, apparently because the latter had a stronger "sound" and did not show the courtesy of interrupting the performance when Dilazenze was going by. Many "racial" conflicts in Brazil happen this way, in discursive fields other than race itself. It is this dismissal of "race" that allows the adepts of *Blocos Afro* to have fun following the *Blocos de Trio* once their Afro parade is over.

25. From the French *mi-carême*, the middle of Lent. These parties occur on weekends after Carnival.

26. Moacir was uncomfortable with the excessive promotion of the trio Jorge Amado/Gabriela/Cacau, because it overlooked the representation of the local Black population's experience. However, the Black population in Ilhéus—at least that which is organized around *candomblé terreiros* and its correlated sociability—only became salient in the decade of the 1930s.

27. Brazilian anthropologist Ana Cláudia Silva, whose simultaneous research with the same population was supervised by Márcio Goldman, was actually researching the hypothesis that the *terreiro* and the *Bloco* might be in the process of becoming a social movement of sorts.

28. In the year of fieldwork, however, the city's cultural administration invited Zebrinha, choreographer of the Ballet Folclórico da Bahia (Salvador) to hold a workshop on Afro Dance. The event contributed to the legitimation of Afro Dance among the dance and ballet academies and provided important training for leaders of Afro groups such as Gleide, from Dilazenze. Gleide would rather say that she practices "ballet Afro," thus upgrading the denomination *dança Afro*.

29. An analysis of *Capoeira* is beyond the scope of this chapter, although it would be a stimulating case in the understanding of disputes around the authority of origins and authenticity. In different phases and contexts, *Capoeira* has been defined as African, as Angolan, as invented by

slaves in Brazil, as a product of the underclasses of Rio (including Portuguese marginals), as specifically Bahian, as the Brazilian national sport, and so on. Today it is undergoing a process of internationalisation. The construction of the Africanness of *Capoeira* is common to all interpretations and highlights the place that Africa occupies in the "philosophy of culture" (Appiah 1992) as an imaginary place where all primordial, physical, sensory, and sensual forces are supposed to dwell, and which late modernity supposedly would be trying to salvage.

30. Third parties are as valid research partners as any others. Unfortunately I wasn't able to include a statement by Adriana Ribeiro.

31. The issue of music goes beyond the scope of this chapter. But it is a fundamental aspect for understanding the notion of cultural "property" among Black groups. See, on the subject, Sansone and Santos (1998).

3
TRISTES LUSO-TROPIQUES:
THE ROOTS AND RAMIFICATIONS
OF LUSO-TROPICALIST
DISCOURSES

Introduction

The journey back home is an integral part of anthropology. The (Afro-) Brazilian experience made me look at Portugal with different eyes: first of all, because I became aware of the prevalence of a Luso-Tropicalism of sorts in Brazilian common sense; and then because I felt uncomfortable with the persistence of an imperial and expansionistic rhetoric in Portugal, even in the discourse on postcolonial identity reconfiguration. This was most obvious during the celebrations of the five hundred years of the Discoveries, particularly of the "Discovery" of Brazil. Furthermore, the expression "Lusophony" has been gaining increasing currency as a device that helps to regain—in both the "spiritual realm" of the cultural products (language, with "Lusophony") and the institutional one, with the CPLP[1]—that which has been lost in the political and material one (Empire as such).

This chapter revolves around three sets of reflections raised by the closure of fieldwork in Brazil. The first one deals with the discursive field called "Luso-Tropicalism": it is seen as having roots and ramifications that are not contained in the Brazilian context or in the work of Gilberto Freyre. I demonstrate this with examples of discourses on Portuguese historical, anthropological, and literary exegesis that were produced as early as the second half of the nineteenth century, during what is known as Decadentism. Furthermore, I analyze discourses and political options that refer us back to the Portuguese colonial period between World War II and the independence of the colonies in the 1970s.

The second set deals with the present importance of the debate on Luso-Tropicalism. Something that may be labeled as "Luso-Tropicalist" resists and reemerges in Brazil, but mostly in Portugal, in the context of identity redefinition in the era of globalization. This is obvious in the Portuguese struggle for a politically correct way of celebrating the Discoveries, in the dealings with Portuguese emigrant communities and with immigrants in Portugal, in the building of a "Lusophone space," and in the debates on the dilemma between European integration and a so-called Atlantic and transnational vocation.

The third set focuses on what could be called the "third level" of discussion on Luso-Tropicalism. If the first level has to do with the constitution of Luso-Tropicalist discourses, and the second with a critique of them with political and material criteria, the third level goes beyond both; a cultural and social approach that denies both culturalism and materialist reductionism may allow us to accept the notion of diversity and specificity in colonial processes, thus enriching postcolonial theory.

As in all reflections of this sort, the personal journey is determining. This chapter is the "logical" consequence of fieldwork in Bahia on the relations between the politics of cultural representation, ethnicity, race, and its embodiments, within the context of emergence of the Black movement. As an anthropologist and Portuguese citizen working in Brazil with Black "informants," all the schemes of representation, interpretation, and ideology that are used in both Brazil and Portugal for the making of discourses on this field have to be reevaluated. One needs to overcome a discourse that is simultaneously anchored in the past and a prisoner of uncontested tropes. One needs to overcome the *tristes* (Luso-)*tropiques*.

Gilberto Freyre and Luso-Tropicalism

Any discussion of Luso-Tropicalism must be based on a reading of Gilberto Freyre's *The Masters and the Slaves* (MS), first published in Brazil in 1933. It was first published in Portugal in 1957, with six subsequent Portuguese editions until 1983. This fact, as the reader will see, is not irrelevant to my argument,[2] based on the circularity of the discourse that links Gilberto Freyre, the bibliography on national formation and identity in both Portugal and Brazil, and the Portuguese colonial ideologies. For that reason my reading of MS focuses on the issues of Portuguese identity and the Portuguese colonial "adventure."

Freyre argues for the "peculiar disposition of the Portuguese for a hybrid and slaveocratic colonization of the Tropics,"[3] which he explains as a result of the Portuguese "ethnic, or rather cultural, past, as a people undefined between Europe and Africa" (1992: 5). Then he defines the Portuguese as marked by "a shaky balance of antagonisms" (1992: 6). The main antagonism would be rooted on the Euro-African mixture, that is, in the ethnically hybrid character of the Portuguese in the pre-Discoveries period. The scarcity of human capital was supposedly overcome during the colonialization process by "extreme mobility and miscegenation" (1992: 8). The Portuguese "joyfully mixed with women of color … and multiplied in mixed children" (1992: 9). The colonial system was based on the slaveocratic and patriarchal family that conveyed a *sui generis* sexual morality, as well as a special version of Catholicism. Portuguese plasticity—which resulted in the synthesis of miscegenation, mobility, and adaptation—led to a process of non-Europeanization of Brazil; this was largely achieved thanks to the Africans' role of cultural mediators.

Freyre's book was to be accused of creating an idyllic image of colonial society, one in which relationships between masters and slaves are not explained in racial and political-economic terms, but rather as a culturalist result of the migration of Iberian family patriarchy to the tropics. Araújo (1994) stresses Freyre's neo-Lamarckian conception of race, thanks to which the category of biological stock as a race definer becomes malleable by the environment. In this sense the bicontinental nature of the Portuguese would have enabled the colonizer to live well with the excesses of the tropical milieu; this, in turn, "would increase the degree of *hybris* that the colonizer had brought along with him" (Luiz Costa Lima, in the introduction to Araújo 1994: 9).

Freyre's modernism was of a regionalist and conservative kind, as opposed to the nationalist and modernizing kind, which was dominant at the time. Freyre's purpose was to break with the latent or explicit racism that characterized a good part of Brazilian discussion of miscegenation until 1933. Two standpoints were then prevalent: the first one said that the country was not viable; the second refused that condemnation and claimed that miscegenation could be seen as whitening, thus redeeming Brazil (Araújo 1994: 29). A third one was Freyre's: it distinguished race from culture and proposed another vision of national identity, one in which the "obsession with progress and reason … is replaced up to a point by an interpretation that considers … the hybrid and peculiar articulation of traditions …" (Araújo 1994: 29). Benzaquen de Araújo's work is one of the most recent contributions to the exegesis of Freyre, an exegesis also of Brazil's origins and the formation of contemporary society, marked by the antinomy between harsh social and racial inequalities on the one hand, and a commonsense discourse that acclaims miscegenation and "racial democracy" on the other. Therefore, the theme of Luso-Tropicalism is not paramount. One can, nevertheless, assert the following: today's discourses on or about the "field of Luso-Tropicalism" are historically anchored on Freyre's masterwork on the patriarchal economy of colonial northeastern Brazil.

Freyre's analysis revolves around a set of criteria: hybrid ethnic origins; mobility, miscegenation, adaptation (*aclimatibilidade*), resulting in plasticity; slaveocratic patriarchalism and *sui generis* Catholicism; and, furthermore, the *hybris*, particularly sexual excess. It seems easy, from today's point of view, to criticize these criteria: Portuguese hybridism does not differ from any other people's hybridism; the three criteria of plasticity (and plasticity itself) are historical precipitates, not cultural essences; and sexual *hybris* naturalizes power in the recesses of the libido, thus desocializing the processes of construction of gender and sexuality.

The point I want to make is different, though: all of those elements are to be found in the representations of Portuguese identity before and after Freyre. One can find them in Portuguese social sciences and literature, in official discourses, and in commonsense identity self-representations with amazing resilience and capacity to adapt to different political situations. That which in Brazil was to become a construction of exceptionality ("racial democracy," "cordiality," "contention of social explosions," etc.) was to become, in Portugal, a construction of exceptionality of the Discoveries and Expansion. Portuguese exceptionalism, as an ideological construct, was actually to increase during the harsher times of the colonial conflict in Africa (1961–1975).

Although the foundations of Luso-Tropicalism are already implicit in MS (1933), the doctrine was not made explicit until Freyre's lecture in Goa in 1951 called *Uma Cultura Moderna: a Luso-tropical* (A Modern Culture: Luso-Tropical). Luso-Tropicalism is developed and explained in *Um Brasileiro em Terras Portuguesas* (A Brazilian in Portuguese Lands, 1955, including the Goa lecture), *Integração Portuguesa nos Trópicos* (Portuguese Integration in the Tropics, 1958), and *O Luso e o Trópico* (The Luso and the Tropic, 1961).

Um Brasileiro em Terras Portuguesas (BTP) is a collection of speeches given between 1951 and 1952 during Freyre's journeys in the Portuguese colonies, as a guest of Portugal's Minister of the Overseas. The book is connected to another, *Aventura e Rotina* (Adventure and Routine), a travel journal of sorts. These books were the object of criticism in both Brazil and Portugal: Freyre was accused of collaborating with Portugal's dictatorial and colonialist regime. He actually acknowledged that criticism, since in BTP he lets the reader know that he had been invited to visit both the Soviet Union and India; the invitations were conveyed to him by Brazilian author Jorge Amado, then a communist intellectual, "precisely when some devotees of the so-called 'left' … accused me— in their delirium of political devotion—to be 'sold out to the fascist Salazar' or to be on 'the pay roll of decadent Portugal'" (Freyre 1955: 11).

In 1952, during a lecture in Coimbra called *Em Torno de um Novo Conceito de Tropicalismo* (On a New Concept of Tropicalism), Freyre resumes his ideas from the Goa lecture in the previous year:

> … I believe that I have found during that journey the expression that I was missing to characterize that sort of Lusitanian civilization that, after being victorious in the tropics, is today still in expansion … The expression—Luso-Tropical—seems to me to reveal the fact that Lusitanian expansion in Africa, Asia, and America shows an obvious inclination, on the part of the Portuguese, to an adaptation to the tropics that is not just based on interest, but is also voluptuous …(1955: 134)

The fact that thank-you speeches directed at Freyre are included in the book constitutes an interesting case of political dialogue. Although the following passage may seem a caricature, it does reveal the political project underneath the event portrayed: it is the salute to Freyre made by a young woman called Constância Baltasar, on behalf of "the Mozambican colored women":

> Brazil, thanks to the colonizing genius of Portugal, has grown and developed until it has reached manhood. It is, in a manner of speech, our older brother and the clear mirror in which Portugal looks at herself, proudly admiring her own work ... how grateful we are to Portugal for the immense work that is being done in favor of our true civilization! We have the religious missions, where we are taught the sublime lessons of the Gospels; we have schools directed by the selfless sisters, where we learn the Portuguese mother tongue and how to accomplish our duty of daughters and tomorrow's mothers; and we have the hospitals where—with evangelical patience—the good doctors teach us how to be good nurses ... This place where we are gathered today is an association of Portuguese Blacks that also helps the task of civilizing the natives and works in cooperation with our governors ... Thus, and with the direct contact that we always have with our civilizers, I believe, Professor Gilberto Freyre, that Portugal's mission to uplift the peoples she administers will not be in vain ...(1955: 264–265)

This quote makes clear the fact that the discursive field of Luso-Tropicalism is built like a game of mirrors played by Portuguese history, the formation of Brazil, and Portuguese colonialism. Such a game is by its nature full of anachronisms, impossible comparisons, and ideology.

The Reception of Luso-Tropicalism in Portugal

How was the Luso-Tropicalist program received in Portugal? According to Castelo (1996),[4] the reception was mixed. On the right wing of the political and ideological spectrum, people such as Osório de Almeida and Manuel Múrias made a nationalistic interpretation, by highlighting the specificity of Portuguese colonization; this position would eventually become the regime's attitude toward Luso-Tropicalism after World War II. On the left, there was more criticism (although never a clear opposition), either by comparing doctrine with historical facts (António Sérgio) or with actual policies in the colonies (Maria Archer). Castelo says that the imperial renaissance of the 1930s and 1940s could not easily accept Freyre's culturalism; it would rather stress the inferiority of Blacks or the superiority of European civilization (a stand taken, respectively, by Armindo Monteiro and Norton de Matos, who was governor of Angola during the First Republic[5]). This indicates one of the "ambiguous fertilities" of Freyre's work: antiracialist in the Boasian sense, on the one hand, but based on a sort of essentialist culturalism on the other.

The great transformation would happen after World War II. Portugal felt tremendous anticolonial pressure and tried to adapt to it. The main events and reactions were: the creation of the United Nations and its charter; anticolonial conferences of Third-World countries (especially in Bandung, Indonesia in 1954); the abolishment of the Colonial Act and the change in colonial denominations from "colonies" and "Empire" to "provinces" and "overseas"; and the creation of a rhetoric of the pluricontinental and pluriracial nature of the nation. Freyre's journey in the colonies took place in 1951, the same year of the constitutional amendment that tried to refresh colonialism with the above-mentioned changes. Freyre's doctrine then became useful for Portuguese diplomacy between the Bandung Conference of 1954 and Portugal's acceptance as a member of the United Nations in 1955.

It was in the academic field, however, that the doctrine was more influential. Adriano Moreira introduced Freyre's ideas in his course on overseas politics at the Instituto Superior de Estudos Ultramarinos (School of Overseas Studies). He was backed up by the acceptance of the Luso-Tropicalist criterion by influential scholars such as geographer Orlando Ribeiro, anthropologist Jorge Dias, and human ecologist Almerindo Lessa (Castelo 1996). Castelo evaluates the repercussions of Luso-Tropicalism in her analysis of the works published in the collection *Estudos de Ciências Políticas e Sociais* (Studies in Social and Political Science). This collection edited by Adriano Moreira and published in 1963, contained fourteen essays on the topic written between 1956 and 1961, by scholars such as Moreira, Narana Coissoró, and Jorge Dias. The beginning of the war in Angola (1961) and the previous invasion/liberation/reintegration (according to different points of view) of Portuguese India led the policy makers to attempt to "luso-tropicalize" overseas legislation and administration. Moreira, head of the Centro de Estudos Políticos e Sociais, introduced some reforms when he took the post of Minister of the Overseas (1960–62): he abolished the Native Status Laws (*Estatuto dos Indígenas*) and promoted administrative decentralization, policies that led to his demise as minister due to the pressure exerted by the integrationist sectors of the regime.

Still, according to Castelo, Salazar and Franco Nogueira (the head of Propaganda) used Luso-Tropicalist discourse in interviews given to the foreign press. The discourse was bound to enter the national imagination, and one can observe how it is being recycled today through the notion of a Lusophone community. But I would go further: my hypothesis is that there was a happy coincidence between Freyre's ideas and something that was already effective in Portuguese national representations.

Portuguese Roots of Luso-Tropicalism

João Leal (2002a) deals with the invention and circulation of stereotypes concerning the "ethnic psychology" in the history of Portuguese anthropology. The year 1950 was a turning point for Jorge Dias with the publication of *Os Elementos Fundamentais da Cultura Portuguesa* (The Fundamental Elements of Portuguese

Culture). In it Dias lists the set of psychological qualities that supposedly define the specificity of Portuguese culture and the expansionistic character of Portuguese temperament, as well as a set of antinomies that are taken to be characteristic of that temperament. Jorge Dias's topics of analysis were not invented *ex-nihilo*. Leal traces their origin back to ethnogenealogical debates about European nations that were first felt in Portugal with the work of Teófilo Braga. In *O Povo Português* (The Portuguese People, quoted by Freyre in MS), published in 1885, Braga lists the ethnic qualities of the Portuguese: excessive pride, mimetic and amorous genius, a nonspeculative character, an inclination toward fatalism, softness of character, adventurous genius, and an inclination toward maritime expansion. The theme of ethnic psychology can also be found in Adolfo Coelho (1993 [1890]). According to Leal, Coelho's work—as was common with many other authors at the turn of the century—had two phases regarding national character: an optimistic one and a pessimistic one. The latter was part and parcel of Decadentism and intellectual reactions to the British Ultimatum.

Decadentism—the complaint of the loss of past glory when the country was compared to industrialized Europe—was countered in the 1910–20 period by a sort of literary criticism (led by poet Teixeira de Pascoaes) that was anticosmopolitan in nature. It revived the nationalistic tendencies of the 1890s that were further stressed by the proclamation of the Republic. Foreign influence was blamed for the country's decline since the Discoveries. *Saudade*, a theme that had been discussed ever since the writings of King Duarte in the Middle Ages, was explained as a contradictory feeling that is specific to Portuguese character. It supposedly connected separate spheres: the Semitic element of *Saudade* as pain, and the Arian element of *Saudade* as desire.

Leal says that Jorge Dias had already dealt with the theme in his 1942—and first—essay, *Acerca do sentimento da natureza entre os povos latinos* (On the sentiment of nature among the Latin peoples). But it is in *Os Elementos...* that Dias explains that the Portuguese "personality" is based on a set of contradictions: between dream and action, kindness and violence, adaptation and ability to safeguard its own character, individual freedom and solidarity, and so on. This paradoxical character would be the explanation for two traits in Portuguese history: alternating periods of grandeur and decline; and the peculiarities of Portuguese expansion (close to Freyre's notion of the "undefined" and "antagonistic" character of the Portuguese).

In 1968, in *O Carácter Nacional Português Na Presente Conjuntura* (Portuguese National Character Today), Dias adds one aspect: he tries to make compatible ethnogenealogical pluralism and the specific capacity for miscegenation (Leal 2002a). Leal wonders whether Freyre's influence was not explicit in this case. The fact is that *Os Elementos...* would become a cult essay: it was republished in the 1990s in wide-circulation pocket editions. The ideas in the essay circulate in Portugal with the same vigor as Freyre's theses do in Brazil: they are both texts whose main theses coincide with national self-representations.

51

Os Elementos… was first presented at the First Symposium of Luso-Brazilian Studies in 1950 in Washington, D. C. Some passages of the essay can be directly compared with some of Gilberto Freyre's assertions:

> [Geographical conditions and original miscegenation:] Portugal is at the natural meeting point of navigation lines between Europe, Africa, and America; her population is made up of the fusion between ethnic elements from the North and the South … a passageway and meeting point for various races. (1950: 142)

> [Expansionistic character:] Portugal was born out of the struggle against the Moors … it seemed that fighting was over … But it wasn't; the Spanish neighbors started coveting Portugal [with the conquest of Ceuta and the beginning of expansion]. From then until today all of Portuguese culture is permeated by maritime and overseas influences. (1950: 144)

> [Plasticity:] The Portuguese has a tremendous capacity to adapt to all things, ideas, and beings, although that does not mean the loss of character. It was this characteristic that allowed him to maintain an attitude of tolerance, and that has given Portuguese colonization its unmistakable character: assimilation through adaptation … (1990: 146). The ability to adapt, the human sympathy, and the amorous temperament are the keys to Portuguese colonization. The Portuguese assimilated by adapting. He has never felt repugnance toward other races and was always relatively tolerant toward other cultures and religions. (1950: 156)

Finally, one of the few—and careful—references to sexual *hybris*: "Portuguese miscegenation does not have a sensual explanation only, although it is characterized by a strong sexuality" (1950: 156). In another text, *Paralelismo de processo na formação das nações* (Parallels in the national formation process), which was presented at a conference at the University of Paraná (Brazil) in 1953 and published in 1956, Jorge Dias asks: "When one looks at Brazil, what does one see?" And he answers:

> A huge country … In 1500 it was officially discovered by the Portuguese who, in subsequent phases, occupied the hinterland and colonized it, in order to obtain the tropical produce that were needed in the European markets … since it was not demographic pressure that pushed the Portuguese toward expansion … scarce population … and precarious health conditions made it necessary to import an ethnic element that could better adapt to the environment … It was then necessary to use the African element … Slavery—something horrible for us today—was then common in Africa; the Portuguese did not invent it. The only innovation was to transport them from one continent to another. (1956: 122–24)

Here explanations that historically contextualize the facts (especially materialistic explanations) seem to be more important than essentialist culturalist generalizations (except, of course, the notion of environmental adaptation by

Africans). But culturalist analysis soon regains center stage: "… Miscegenation started from the onset. In those times of danger and insecurity colonization was done only by men who, since they had no white women, were attracted to women of other races" (1956: 123). And on the following page he presents his theoretical groundings, which would not have been challenged by Freyre:

> There are three basic elements in the formation of a culture: land, Man, and tradition. The land is the natural frame, made up of the soil, the climate, the animal and plant resources, and so on, that are available for Man's provision of his primary needs, as well as of the secondary ones that result from the former. Man is the ethnic element, the so-called *race*, with special aptitudes and characteristics, developed throughout millennia of prehistory and which have most probably been fixed late in his biological evolution. Finally, tradition is the ensemble of knowledge, inclinations, tastes, and so on, that Man has developed throughout centuries or millennia of struggle against the natural elements… (1956: 124)

Ethnogenealogy and National Character

If, as Leal demonstrated, Jorge Dias's notions are rooted in ethnogenealogical speculation and in ethnic psychology (and they meet Freyre's Luso-Tropicology at some point), they are for both authors rooted in interpretations grounded in culturalist anthropology: "race" is replaced by "ethnic (group)"; they are also based on dominant interpretations of the history of Portugal and Portuguese expansion. As an example of this, let us consider the foreword to Freyre's *O Mundo que o português criou* (The world the Portuguese made, 1951) written by António Sérgio—a socialist and positivist historian who could hardly be accused of nationalistic fantasies. Sérgio starts by saying that "…It is not surprising that the readers transition from the problem of the Portuguese in Brazil to the problem of the Portuguese in Portugal, and that some will feel inclined to use in the latter the reverse solution that Freyre provided for the former" (Sérgio 1951: 10). After an abstract of Freyre's theory on *miscibilidade, mobilidade,* and *aclimabilidade,* Sérgio recalls an essay titled *O colonizador português e o seu carácter* (The Portuguese colonizer and his character) by Almir de Andrade (in *Aspectos da Cultura Brasileira*). The Brazilian author mentioned the "anti-European" psychological and social formation of the Portuguese. Referring to the Portuguese maladjustment to the European environment, he said that "maybe that maladjustment explains that movement of decadence and weakening that has filled more than four centuries of Portugal's history." Furthermore, "their qualities as colonizers and their defects as a European nation were one and the same thing" (1951: 13, quoted by Sérgio). Sérgio then asks, "When we say that the Portuguese people cannot adapt to European culture, aren't we denying the spiritual plasticity that we first saw as the cause for adaptation in the tropics? … If we are plastic how can we be anti-

European?" (Sérgio 1951: 15). He is suggesting not only an incompatibility between Almir de Andrade and Freyre, but also the contradictory nature of arguments that make general statements about a people's personality once they are confronted with historical facts. Sérgio explains, then, how the Portuguese problem is rooted in the physical impossibility of having a basic staple agriculture, thus finding in commerce and navigation the economic alternative. His argument goes on to environmental and geographical factors until, on page 22, he adds problems of another sort: those that have to do with the socio-economic structure of the people: "That is why before we start attributing intrinsic qualities to the decadence of our people today, it might be wiser to think of the social consequences that are the outcome of the low purchasing power of the majority of the people" (Sérgio 1951: 23). It is in the unraveling of his interpretation of the social and economic history that Sérgio strikes the final blow: "Would that not be an acceptable explanation for the decadence of the people at home, thus leaving aside the hypothesis of the nebulous psyche of our people?" (Sérgio 1951: 25).

The argument of the nebulous psyche seems to be resilient, however. Eduardo Lourenço in *Psicanálise mítica do povo português* (Mythical psychoanalysis of the Portuguese people, 1978) stresses how the nineteenth century was marked by the question

> … whether we were still viable given the obvious decadence. Between Herculano's or Garrett's youth and the generation of Antero there is the industrial and cultural revolution of the nineteenth century, the echoes of which were heard in the patriotic criticism of the 1870 generation…. In order to escape that negative image of itself, Portugal discovers Africa. (1978: 27)

According to Lourenço, the British Ultimatum and the reactions to it gave room for the blooming of "the nastiest flower of patriotic love—nationalistic mysticism" (1978: 28). That was a form of reaction to the powerless and devastating criticism of the 1870s, as well as to the aggression of the "civilized monster" (Britain). *Saudosismo* was to translate that nationalism, while the so-called Portuguese philosophy (connected to the poetics of the above-mentioned Pascoaes) was to make the apology of the "incomparable excellence of being Portuguese" (Lourenço 1978: 37) against the humanist liberalism of the 1870s. The result was "the making of a scary cultural and historical myth that claimed as specific an identity that many other peoples in other places and times had claimed" (Lourenço 1978: 39). This led to a culturalist praising of Portugal on the basis of empire. It also led to a historiographic fixation on the period of the Discoveries, and not only on the right wing of the ideological spectrum, but also among historians such as Jaime Cortesão, Duarte Leite, and Vitorino Magalhães Godinho.

Godinho wrote the 1964 preface to Jaime Cortesão's *Os Factores Democráticos na Formação de Portugal* (The Democratic Factors in the Formation of Portugal). According to him, the *História da Colonização Portuguesa do Brasil* (History of the Portuguese Colonization of Brazil) edited by Malheiro Dias (1921–22) had revealed Cortesão as a historian in a Portugal that was fresh out of a war it had fought for the preservation of the overseas "that had been threatened by industrial and capitalist imperialism and with the purpose of defending true human values with which to build the Portuguese community in the four corners of the world" (Godinho 1964: 7). Portugal was also getting ready to take part in the celebration of the one hundredth anniversary of Brazil's independence. In 1922 President António José de Almeida was received in Rio by Ambassador Duarte Leite (also an author of the *História da Colonização ...*), and Cortesão was part of the cultural mission that went with him. Cortesão was to go into exile in 1927, and wrote *Os Factores ...* in 1930, under the influence of Brunhes' human geography, Pirenne's economic and social history, and Durkheim's sociology. In sum: the historian that was to be considered as the Portuguese representative of the Annales school *avant la lettre* also wrote in an essay in *Os Factores ...* ("*Causas da independência de Portugal e da formação portuguesa do Brasil*"—Causes of the independence of Portugal and of the Portuguese formation of Brazil) that

> The Portuguese, whose national character was shaped during the first centuries of his history, was raised by two schools: the school of chivalry with its discipline, directed against Islam; and the school of Franciscanism. These are the roots of his action as a discovering and colonizing people ... the chivalrous spirit is common to the Portuguese and the Spanish. But Franciscanism makes the former different ... Those Brazilian, as well as Portuguese qualities of cordial fraternity, tolerance and forgiveness, optimism, generous and youthful effusion, and down-to-earth simplicity, are rooted in Franciscan Christianity ... (1930: 183)

This example shows how, in the historiography of the Discoveries, interpretations based on economic and social criteria could go hand in hand with statements about the national character. This line of thought was not very different from the so-called sociology of the formation of Brazil, which was contemporary to Portuguese debates on national character and the fundamental elements of the Portuguese culture.

Evaldo Cabral de Melo, in his afterword to *Raízes do Brasil* (Roots of Brazil) by Sérgio Buarque de Holanda (1936), criticizes the notion of sociology of the formation of Brazil. He says that "the morbid and narcissistic inclination toward settling accounts with the national past is an intellectual fad that has been passed on to Brazil and Hispanic America from the Iberian Peninsula" (1936: 191). He was referring to the so-called 1930s generation: Sérgio Buarque, Caio Prado Júnior, and Gilberto Freyre.

Colonial Politics and Policies

Let us now turn to the late colonial context, during which Freyre's work was to circulate with greater political compromise in Portugal—as well as in the academic milieu as part of the game of mirrors between Brazilian and Portuguese

55

intellectual elites. According to Rui Pereira (1986), until 1955 Portuguese anthropological research in the colonies was circumscribed to the biological anthropology studies conducted by the Oporto school, whose journeys into the field had started in 1935. The so-called overseas ethnology started with Jorge Dias's team's work in the Missões de Estudos das Minorias Étnicas do Ultramar (Overseas Ethnic Minorities Study Mission), which was created in 1957. The Centro de Estudos Políticos e Sociais was in charge of the missions. The center was determined to break away from the sort of biological anthropology research done by the Centro de Estudos de Etnologia do Ultramar, which had been founded under the aegis of the Instituto Superior de Estudos Ultramarinos and the Junta de Investigações do Ultramar (Pereira 1986).

Pereira establishes the beginning of the Portuguese colonial enterprise at a date coinciding with the foundation of the Sociedade de Geografia de Lisboa (Lisbon Geographical Society) in 1875. The earliest indication of a perceived need for dealing with native customs is Angola in 1911–12: after the creation of the Ethnological Museum of Angola and the Congo, governor Norton de Matos (1912–15) established the Serviço dos Negócios Indígenas (Native Affairs Service) in 1913. During his second term of office (1921–23) he created the Secretaria de Colonização e Negócios Indígenas (Department of Colonization and Native Affairs), already with the purpose of promoting colonial settlements; and the focus on ethnographic studies was replaced with the promotion of a large congress of Tropical Medicine.

After the 1926 coup and the establishment of the *Estado Novo*, colonial policy was rationalized. In a first phase, until World War II and under the leadership of Salazar, the meager development of the colonies was curtailed and frozen in order to overcome the 1929 crisis. The situation was reversed due to the need for import substitution during World War II. After the war, the UN Charter of 1945 and the Bandung Conference of non-aligned countries ten years later, the *Estado Novo* had to react to anti-colonial pressure. The 1951 Constitution revoked the Colonial Act of 1930: the colonies were renamed "Overseas Provinces," and the objectives of Assimilation and Integration (of the native populations) was established. The colonial populations were henceforth divided in three strata: colonials, assimilated and natives (Pereira 1986).

According to this anthropologist, the *Estado Novo* had to rethink the relationship between colonizers and colonized in order to avoid nationalist movements. That was how JIU (Junta de Investigações do Ultramar, Overseas Research Board) "embraced Malinowski's teachings" (Pereira 1986: 219) with a thirty-year delay. The above-mentioned missions were part of this policy. Jorge Dias, who was in charge of them, was faced with the colonial reality; this led him to reevaluate his beliefs regarding the Portuguese colonial administration. From the mission report of 1957, Pereira highlights this sentence by Dias: "Blacks ... fear us ... and when they compare us with other whites they always do so unfavorably for us" (1957: 59 in Pereira 1986: 223). The following passage is even more revealing:

... We are told time and time again that the natives prefer the Portuguese to the English because we treat them more humanely and take interest in their lives. This tale is repeated just like some errors pass on from one book to another,[6] because the authors prefer to repeat what others have said instead of checking the accuracy of the information ... (quoted in Pereira 1986: 224)

Note that the year was 1959, a few years after Freyre's travels in the colonies (1951–52); the written results were published in 1955. In the same 1959 report, Dias also wrote:

... A double inversion seems to have occurred in the traditional attitudes of racial behavior on both sides of the Rovuma. While we, who are still considered the least prejudiced people due to our nature and tradition, have been deforming that tradition in northern Mozambique, the English are the cause of even greater surprise in Tanganyika, with their policy of multiracial understanding. (1959: 8 in Pereira 1986: 226)

Pereira says that this passage was a harsh blow on the regime's love for the Luso-Tropicalism defined by Freyre in 1958 in *Integração Portuguesa nos Trópicos* (Portuguese Integration in the Tropics), published by JIU and by the Center presided by Adriano Moreira). Jorge Dias actually said in 1957 that "many of those in charge who live in the area believe that we will not be around twenty years from now" (1957: 58 in Pereira 1986: 203). He was right. Armed struggle began in the region in 1964, three years after it had started in Angola—when Adriano Moreira was Minister of the Overseas. It was precisely at this juncture—marked by the first real attempts at colonization and colonial development on the one hand, and by the beginning of the liberation movements on the other—that Luso-Tropicalism became useful in helping transform the representations and practices of the anachronistic Portuguese colonialism.

What did Freyre say in his 1958 *Integração Portuguesa nos Trópicos*? The essay was published in the first issue of the journal *Estudos de Ciências Políticas e Sociais*, edited by Adriano Moreira (the issue's theme was overseas policy). Freyre starts by invoking Evans-Pritchard's authority. The British anthropologist had told Freyre that he agreed with the notion of a "Hispanic- and Christ-centric constant [in what we would call Portuguese colonialism] instead of European ethnocentric [in what we would call British colonialism]" (Freyre 1958: 20). In a reference to the political context (the Portuguese regime's notion that both Soviet and American imperialisms were behind anticolonial pressures), Freyre says:

... The articulation of Luso-Tropical civilizations in a transnational system of culture, economy, and politics is a necessity, not so much in geopolitical terms but rather—considering other so-called geopolitical expansions—as an articulation that is the natural outcome of natural and geographical situations ... We believe that the unofficial anticolonial policy of the U.S. (i.e., of some of its politicians in Africa and the East) is an excuse for preparing American political and economic domination in the tropical areas that are still under European influence … and where Luso-Tropical cultures and societies similar to Brazil are being formed, as in Angola or Mozambique. (1958: 27)

This geostrategic concern is to be found in Adriano Moreira's arguments and in his tentative modernization of colonial ideology. If in Freyre's *O Luso e o Trópico* (1961) the 1958 argument is repeated, it is, however, in a marginal essay that we can find a more politically engaged approach. As a matter of fact, in 1963 Freyre gave a speech at the Gabinete Português de Leitura in Rio, as a guest of the Federation of Portuguese Associations of Brazil, on Portugal's national day. Once again he stressed the politically independent nature of his journey to the Portuguese colonies (he also repeated the story of the invitations to visit Eastern European countries), and commented on the political solidarity between two countries with opposed political regimes—Portugal and Brazil:

> Solidarity … is not political … It reaches deeper than that. It reaches down to the roots. It projects itself apolitically into the future. It has to do with the fact that we make up a socio-cultural ensemble that is characterized by traditions, trends, and destinies that are common to Portugal and to the groups of descendants of Portuguese who are more or less deeply integrated in tropical environments, Brazil being today the most expressive case. (Freyre 1963: 8)

After saying that Portugal is no longer European (and implicitly admitting the image of multicontinental Portugal upheld by the regime in its final phase), he went on to describe the Luso-Tropical traits that he cherished as the foundations for a community that was to be more Luso-Tropical than specifically Luso-Brazilian: "… it is the inclination toward miscegenation in the biological level, and the enrichment of the Portuguese language with tropicalisms" (1963: 10). Later on, he wondered how "can one accept as fair the campaign that has been waged in the last two years [i.e., since the beginning of the colonial wars] … against Portugal … and which has had reflections in Brazil too?"[7] (1963: 12). Although he validated Basil Davidson's criticism when he said that in Angola only 1 percent of natives were "assimilated" (that is, able to have access to citizenship), he said that the same could be said of Brazil regarding the Indians. But what Freyre insisted on stressing—in an argument where comparisons fail—is that patriarchalism in Angola was *assimilating* just like it did in Brazil. He accepted that there could have been more modern methods for achieving that end but he was seduced by the tale of the white farmer who confessed to him that he had beaten his Black servant—but a servant whom he called by his Christian name and not as a "boy"; and he suggested that this sort of thing should be promoted in the United States, where parents have no discipline over their children. This is summarized later in the essay in ways similar to *The Masters and the Slaves* thirty years before:

It is thanks to the patriarchal methods of integration of primitive peoples into sociologically Christian systems of common living that the Portuguese were able to add the democracy of miscegenation to the necessary authoritarianism of the patriarchal family system, [thus creating] … Brazil—maybe the largest, the most authentic and complete racial democracy that the world has yet seen. (Freyre 1963: 12)

The Colonial Conundrum

I have already mentioned that Adriano Moreira, besides having been a major figure in the political and social sciences of the late colonial period, was also Minister of the Overseas between 1960 and 1962.[8] During a speech as minister, in 1961, and while talking about the settlement policies directed at Portuguese soldiers who had been drafted in the beginning of the colonial war, he said that

> … We want to make it clear to the commonwealth of nations our national decision to pursue a policy of multiracial integration, without which there will be neither peace nor civilization in Black Africa … it is a policy whose benefits are proven by the largest country of the future, Brazil …(Moreira 1961: 10–11)

Nevertheless, he felt that the Native Status Laws were misunderstood, because "It was due to a simple concern for authenticity that our Native Status Laws denied the natives the political rights to such institutions [of sovereignty], but people accused us of denying them citizenship/nationality" (1961: 12). He had previously stated that

> Since the main rationale for the Status Laws lies in the respect for the private lives of the several ethnic groups, we conclude that it is opportune to revise those laws, so that it is clearly understood by all that the Portuguese people lives under a political law that is equal for everyone, with no racial, religious or cultural privilege. (1958: 14)

And he finished his speech by saying that the revision of those laws did not mean that one forgot the "missionary" work that they stood for. On the contrary, one was entering the phase of "Portugueseness for all," in order to settle the territories with integrated multiracial communities.

In his *Contribuição de Portugal para a valorização do homem no Ultramar* (Portugal's contribution to the uplifting of Man overseas, 1958), he refused to accept the notion of conflict that underlay anticolonial theories, for it did not leave room for human dignity and "polarizes White man and Black man, forgetting the universalistic and humanistic message of the Discoveries" (1958: 12). How could Moreira legitimate this statement? He did so by saying that

> The great sociologist Gilberto Freyre is right when he notes that in Toynbee's oppositional classification of civilizations that peculiar way of being in the world that

he fortunately named Luso-Tropical is missing … It was this conception of egalitarian life, of human democracy, that was the most significant contribution of Portuguese action in the world … absolutely oblivious to notions of conflict and domination, or to the feeling of racial superiority or inferiority … (1958: 13)

In order to further sustain his argument, he quoted Jorge Dias, who said that the

relationship of great cordiality that we were able to establish … is explained by the special formation of Portuguese society. The Portuguese family, of a multifunctional patriarchal type … (which survives today in spite of individualism …) explains this system of fraternal relationships between masters and dependents. (1958: 14)

Although Moreira did not provide the reader with the references he used, he claimed that Jorge Dias wrote that "when we used slave labor, we often included slaves in our patriarchal, multifunctional family, like some Brazilian authors have highlighted" (Dias in Moreira 1958: 14). We also do not know to which authors Dias was referring, but the list would certainly include Freyre. Referring to "the unpublished work on the Portuguese integration in the tropics," Moreira said that Freyre would have agreed with his definition of a sense of universality in Portuguese culture—a culture that is alien to conflict. The sense of cordiality would come from this:[9] "It is a quality opposed to all ethnocentrism, which is the basis for attitudes that value the black man, the yellow man, the mulatto man or the white man, thus forgetting the common dignity of all …" (1958: 16). Now note the coincidence between Freyre's (1958) phrasing (see quotation above) and the following passage. I have not been able to find out who quotes whom: "We believe that the unofficial anticolonial policy of the U.S. (i.e., of some of its politicians in Africa and the East) is an excuse for preparing American political and economic domination in the tropical areas …" (1958: 17). Assimilation—a political concept of the colonial administration—was portrayed as an ancient characteristic of Portuguese expansionism. It was promoted, supposedly, as a way toward cultural interpenetration, as a negation of ethnocentrism (which contradicts the notion of ethnic separation based on the respect for specificity), and based on the principle that "it is cultures, not races, that are eternal" (Moreira 1958: 20). It was based on this premise that Moreira was in favor of interracial marriage, alleging that the family is the best instrument in the creation of equal multiracial societies. It was only due to a lapse of memory (sometimes on purpose, he adds) that "some critics ignore that the traditional Portuguese system was the first instance of a system of effective rights, only to be found later in the modern Universal declarations" (1958: 22). A few years earlier, however, in *Problemas Sociais do Ultramar* (1960), the former minister was capable of an analysis that was not mere ideology. Colonial reality was divided into the city and the frontier. In the latter one could find "foreign aggression" (the liberation movements) and in the former one could find "rural exodus" and a concentration of "detribalized" people. A very sensitive issue needed to be addressed: "that of the relationship between Portugueseness and Christianity, not only from a political but also from a cultural point of view." According to him, the experience of exclusive option for total assimilation—which was the rule—and the experience of an optional regime of partial assimilation that followed,

> demonstrate that the method is not good for the needed coincidence between juridical status and cultural status … miscegenation originates a problem, too… there are fewer mixed families than in the past … because the deficit of white women has been reduced. Now *mestiços* tend to make up closed demographic groups, which is not beneficial for integration. (Moreira 1958: 154)[10]

In essays such as *Congregação Geral das Comunidades Portuguesas* (1964) or *Para uma convergência luso-brasileira* (1968), Moreira faced a problem similar to that felt by Jorge Dias in *Estudos do Carácter Nacional* … and the afterword to *Os Elementos* … : what should be done about Portuguese emigrants who, instead of choosing the colonies, choose to go to industrialized countries in Europe and America? Dias feared that the national character might be lost in the process; Moreira thought that emigration was an opportunity to divulge Portuguese colonial attitudes and civilization. Both thought that the problem was the growing hegemony of the United States and what we would today call globalization.

Contemporary Debates

Eduardo Lourenço's 1978 essay was already a reflection on postcolonial Portugal as a nation that did not seem to react traumatically to the loss of its colonies. It was too early, however, for Lourenço to assess the relevance that Europeanism was to achieve in the 1990s or to predict the growing rhetoric around Lusophony; or, still, the commemorative events around the Portuguese Discoveries, and the sort of clash between ingrained Luso-Tropicalism and revisionism in the interpretations that were made. João Leal (2002a) mentions that Lourenço (in the symposium *Existe uma cultura Portuguesa?* (Is there a Portuguese culture?, 1993), used the ideas in Dias's *Os Elementos* … as an argument against anthropologists who answered that question with a no or a maybe.

Boaventura Sousa Santos, too, in *Onze teses* …. (1994b), treated Jorge Dias's work as the most representative of what he calls "mythical discourses on Portugal." Leal says that Dias's essay is so resilient and strong that Sousa Santos's criticism ends up being more nominal than real. In fact, Santos goes on to do a sort of sociological reification of Jorge Dias's theses. Also, in *Modernidade, Identidade e Cultura de Fronteira* (Santos 1994a), Leal does not find such a great difference between Santos's characterization of Portuguese culture as "a border/frontier culture" and some theses in *Os Elementos* … .

In the context of contradictory pressures between global culture and national or regional cultures, Sousa Santos asks who it is that sustains the new or renewed tension between *demos* and *ethnos?*, and he answers:

> ... I think it is culture... . First, Portuguese culture is not just the culture of the Portuguese and vice versa ... Secondly, the specific openings for Portuguese culture are, on the one hand, Europe, and on the other, Brazil—and up to a point, Africa. Thirdly, Portuguese culture is the culture of a country that occupies a semiperipheral position in the world system. (Santos 1994a:130)

In *Modernidade* ... , Sousa Santos quotes himself in *Onze teses* ... where he had attacked the "excessive mythical interpretation" in Portuguese intellectual production. Alternatively, he now says that one must seek to "define the identity status of Portuguese culture and analyze the points of contact with the cultural identities of Brazilian and African peoples. My hypothesis is that Portuguese culture has no content" (1994a: 132). When he analyses the fact that the Portuguese state did not comply with its functions of differentiation and homogenization, he adds, "in symbolic terms, Portugal was too close to its colonies to be wholly European and too far from Europe to be a true colonizer" (1994a:133). Thus, processes of incorporation, mimesis, syncretism, and translocalism, with a deficit of differentiation and identification, would characterize Portugal. Supposedly the reverse of this would be the consolidation of a very specific cultural form—the border (or frontier). The sort of anthropophagy that Oswald de Andrade saw in Brazilian culture would also apply to Portuguese culture in its cosmopolitan aspects. Furthermore,

> Faithful to its semiperipheral nature, Portuguese culture extended the border/frontier zone to the colonies, thus allowing them to use Portugal as the point of passage to central cultures ... The global context of the return of identity, of multiculturalism, of transnationalization and localization seems to offer unique opportunities ... Will they be seized? (Santos 1994: 135)

Final Remarks

Luso-Tropicalism was never a theory or a school of thought. It was born within a tradition of culturalist essay writing. It was produced by and produced discourses in the field of identity, specificity, and exceptionalism. And it was so both in Brazil and Portugal.

The Brazilian social dynamics—especially in what concerns race and ethnicity—could easily delegitimize Luso-Tropicalism. In Portugal the same could be done by the crisis that put an end to colonialism and the authoritarian regime that supported it and was supported by it. On both sides of the Atlantic, social science became more international. We are now at the point where the research agendas of international social science allow for the theme of Luso-Tropicalism to be a relevant topic of research.

On one hand, something that we could call generic Luso-Tropicalism remains alive—as an inclination, a commonsense interpretation, sometimes as official representation, even when critical discourse becomes stronger (as with the case of the commemorations of the Portuguese Discoveries in the late 1990s). Luso-Tropicalism has become a social fact. On the other hand, some historical and social facts that inspired Luso-Tropicalism remain valid: the undeniable fact of the specificity of Portuguese expansion, of the colonization of Brazil, of the formation of Brazilian society, and so on.

This specific reality should be studied within comparative colonial studies. It may enrich a field that is marked by the context of its production, which is predominantly Anglo-Saxon. Three concerns should be taken into account, however: critical attention to the resilience of Luso-Tropicalism under the guise of Lusophony and its avatars; complex understanding of cultural transits and traffics (Europe, the Americas, Africa), thus overcoming a Lusocentric perspective; and comparison with other colonial and postcolonial cases.

We need to overcome the more psychological, culturalist, and essentialist aspects of Luso-Tropicalism. If we do so we will be able to deal with what matters: the construction of a complex world of meanings and powers by Portuguese, Brazilians, and Africans. Luso-Tropicalism was a discourse permeated with political power and ideological rhetoric: we need to unravel these in order not to reify, once more, "communities" that do not exist as essences.

Notes

1. Commonwealth of Portuguese-Speaking Countries.
2. *Casa-Grande e Senzala. Formação da família brasileira sob o regime da economia patriarcal*, vol. 1 of *Introdução à História da Sociedade Patriarcal no Brasil*, 1933. I have used the 1992 Brazilian edition. American edition: *The Masters and the Slaves*, 1956, New York: Knopf.
3. My translation. The same applies to the rest of the quotations from Portuguese authors.
4. I have used the author's M. A. thesis, not the book, which was published in 1998. The original version of this chapter was written before Castelo's (1998) excellent book was published. Some of the data supplied by that historian were included, since I was able to have access to her thesis (of which her book is the published version), but still does not do her justice. My anthropological interpretation of the facts and discourses of Luso-Tropicalism should be complemented with the reading of Castelo.
5. Monarchy was overthrown in 1910. The First Republic, a formally democratic regime, lasted until 1926, when a military coup established a dictatorship that was to last until 1974. Portugal's African colonies became independent in 1975. In 1986 Portugal joined the European Union.
6. The Luso-Tropicalist theme is endlessly reproduced in travel guides and literature, pop culture, and so on.
7. It is interesting to recall that liberation movements in the Portuguese colonies (especially the life and work of Amilcar Cabral in Guinea-Bissau) were a source of motivation for the Black movement in Brazil.

8. With an education in law, he started working at the Colonial School in 1948. In 1954 he finished his thesis on "The Overseas Prison Problem." He was a member of the Portuguese delegation to the UN between 1957 and 1959; a member of the Chamber of Corporations; Dean of the Instituto Superior de Ciências Sociais e Políticas Ultramarinas; Under-secretary of Overseas Administration, and Minister of the Overseas from 1960 to 1962. He was a founding member and director of the Centro de Estudos Políticos of the Junta de Investigações do Ultramar. He was president of the Lisbon Geographical Society in 1964. He was exiled in Brazil for some time after the restoration of democracy in 1974. After his return to Portugal he was president of CDS (the right-wing Christian Democratic Party) and a member of Parliament. He works on international politics in a military institute focused on issues of national defense.

9. Note that "cordiality" is a frequent trope in Brazilian representations of national identity: the "cordial man" is the foundation of "cordial racism."

10. Since those assimilated and urban mixed groups could constitute nationalistic elites.

4
"Longing for Oneself": Hybridism and Miscegenation in Colonial and Postcolonial Portugal

Foreword

The argument in this chapter acknowledges that hybridism is today a central issue of debate in the social sciences, in a troubling reminiscence of the nineteenth century debate on race and the hybrids. The term "hybrid" was transposed from botany to anthropology and was associated with both political and scientific speculations on "races" as species or subspecies. The acknowledgment of the common humanity of all "races" strengthened the separation between culture and nature as part and parcel of the project of modernity (see Latour 1994); but it also diverted attention from hybridism to the field of miscegenation and *mestiçagem*[1]—that is, "racial" and cultural mixing. Hybridism—and mixing in general—was condemned by some for its impurity and praised by others for its humanism. The result of the century-long debate is, however, much more hybrid itself than a clear opposition. Discourses on miscegenation and *mestiçagem* tended to be used as ideological masks for relations of power and domination. They were also used as central elements in national, colonial, and imperial narratives. The Brazilian case is well known. The Portuguese case is one of the most complex and intriguing: if the "building of Brazil" has been systematically praised as the example of the humanistic and miscegenating characteristic of Portuguese expansion, it has also been used as an argument for the legitimization of later colonialism in Africa, as well as for the construction of a self-representation of the Portuguese as nonracists.

The Portuguese nation, however, has seldom been described as miscegenated and *mestiça* itself. In the discourses of national identity, emphasis has been placed on what the Portuguese have given to others—a gift of "blood" and culture—not on what they have received from others. Present rhetoric on hybridism—as part of globalization, transnationality, postcolonial diasporas, and multiculturalism—clashes with the reality of the return of "race" in cultural fundamentalism, policies of nationality and citizenship, and the politics of representation. This chapter will focus on discourses and modes of classification as the starting point for discussing specific practices and processes of identity dispute in the "Lusophone" space. Three periods in the Portuguese discussion of miscegenation and hybridism will be analyzed: a period marked by racist theories; a period marked by Luso-Tropicalism; and the present period marked by multiculturalism. Finally, the acknowledgment of creolized social formations as both the outcome of colonialism and possible sources for imagining new, less racist societies, closes this exploratory chapter.

Hybris and Monsters

The *Dicionário Moraes* of 1891 refers to *hybrido* as originating in the Greek *hybris,* defined as "an animal generated by two species. Irregular, anomalous, monstrous."[2] *Hybridação* is the "production of hybrid plants or animals" and *hybridez* is the "quality … of that which is composed of two different species"; in grammar it is used to refer to "words compounded from two different languages." The same dictionary does not have an entry for *miscigenação,* but it does for *mestiço,* from the Latin *mixtus,* defined as "that which proceeds from parents of different race or species: e.g., among men (*sic*) the *mulato,* the *cafusa,* etc.; among animals, the mule, etc. It is also used to refer to some grafted plants, e.g., *rosas mestiças.*"

In the *Dicionário Etimológico da Língua Portuguesa* (1952), we learn that the Greek root *hybris* defines "excess, all that exceeds measure; pride, insolence; excessive ardor, impetuousness, exaltation; outrage, insult, offence; violence over woman or child; via the Latin *hybrida* to designate the product of the crossing between the sow and the wild boar; the child of parents from different regions or conditions, probably via the French *hybride.*" In the same dictionary one can already find an entry for *miscigenação,* "from the English *miscegenation,* which came from the Latin *miscere,* 'to mix' + *genus,* 'race.'" After 1960 *miscigenar* is said to mean simultaneously "to procreate hybrids" and "to procreate *mestiços.*" *Mestiço* is said to come from the Castilian *mistizo,* which comes from the Late Latin *mixticiu.* As a complement to this list of definitions, we can also find that the word *mulato* comes from " … *mulo* (male mule)." According to literary examples used in the entry, one can infer (although not prove) that it is in the 1500s—the "Age of Discoveries"—that the animal reference is replaced by a human one.

If one uses the several entries in the *Dicionário de Sinónimos* from Porto Editora, a constellation of meanings connecting these different expressions can be traced: "Híbrido: ambígeno, anómalo, irregular, mestiço, monstruoso (…) Mestiçagem: hibridismo, mestiçamento, miscigenação (…) Mestiço: bode, caboclo, cabra, carafuzo, cariboca, híbrido, mesclado, misto, mulato … Mulato: bode, cabra, cabranaz, cabrito, cabrocha, caporro, escuro, fulo, mestiço, moreno, mu, mulo, pardo, trigueiro … Mulata: cabrita, china, mestiça, mista, morocha, mula, trigueira."[3]

Postcolonial Hybrids

The above-mentioned words are ominous. Accusations of impurity, animalism and illegitimacy are embedded in the semantics and remain so even today; mixed categories are presented as negative (or, at best, ambiguous) consequences of sex and procreation outside the hierarchical and classificatory order. One can sense their construction during the colonial confrontation and encounter. Robert Young (1995) starts his argument with the contention that class, gender, and "race" are promiscuously related to one another, and have become mutually defining metaphors. Colonial desire would be like a hidden but insistent obsession with interracial, transgressive sex, as well as with hybridism and miscegenation (Young 1995: 5). Both language and sex have produced hybrid forms (Creoles, *pidgins*, mixed children, etc.). The word "hybrid" itself, which in the nineteenth century was used to refer to a physiological phenomenon, is reactivated in the twentieth century for describing a cultural one. According to Young (1995) the 1828 *Webster* defined a hybrid as "a mongrel or mule; an animal or plant produced from the mixture of two species." It is only in the 1861 edition of the *Oxford English Dictionary* (OED) that the term is first used to denote the crossing of people of different "races," thus marking the acceptance of the possibility of human hybrids. The 1890 OED actually makes explicit the link between the linguistic (and cultural) and the racial: "The Aryan languages present such indications of hybridity as would correspond with … racial intermixture" (in Young 1995).

Moving from etymology to theory, the problem becomes even more explicit in the entry for *hybridity* in the dictionary of postcolonial studies by Ashcroft et al. (1998). Seen as one of the most used and disputed terms in the field of postcolonial studies, hybridity is usually used to refer to the creation of new transcultural forms in the colonial contact zone. Retracing the use of the expression, Young shows that Bakhtin used it to indicate the potential for transfiguration in multivocal linguistic situations. Today's use of the term, however, is associated with Homi Bhabha, whose analysis of the colonizer/colonized relationship stresses the interdependence and mutual construction of their subjectivities. Cultural identity would always emerge in a "third space of enunciation" (Bhabha 1994: 37), a contradictory and ambivalent space that makes obsolete notions about the purity of cultures and their hierarchy.

Instead of the exoticism of cultural diversity, the focus should be on acknowledging an empowering hybridism (Ashcroft et al. 1998: 118).

This clearly goes beyond the current use of hybridism to describe mere cultural exchange and mixture without taking into account the power inequality in the two parties in a relationship; it also overcomes the use of the term to describe expressions of syncretism, cultural synergy and transculturation. Ashcroft et al. wisely stress this point: "the assertion of a shared postcolonial condition such as hybridity has been seen as part of the tendency of discourse analysis to de-historicize and de-locate cultures from their … contexts …" (1998: 119). Other reservations can be expressed: the term hybridism was influential in imperial and colonial discourses when the union of different "races" was referred to in negative terms (Young 1995). Hybridism became part of the colonial discourse of racism in the late nineteenth and early twentieth centuries. Although the term's ancestry can hardly be considered noble, there is nonetheless a difference between unconscious processes of hybrid mixing (or creolization) and a conscious, politically motivated concern with the deliberate challenging of homogeneity. Young reminds us that for authors such as Bakhtin, hybridism (or, more exactly, "hybridization") was seen as politicized and contestatory. Bakhtin's hybridism "sets different points of view against each other in a conflictual structure, which retains a certain elemental, organic energy and openendedness" (Young 1995: 21–22). This is precisely the notion that Bhabha reclaims: that of the colonized who challenges the authenticity claimed by the colonizer.

Young confirms what I have previously said: hybridism is becoming a key subject in the cultural debates of the late twentieth and early twenty-first centuries, similar to what happened in the late nineteenth century. The discussion then was focused on the political and cultural consequences of the scientific theory of the differences between species for humankind. The generally accepted test was that of the infertility of the offspring of sexual unions between different species. But infertility was not sufficient as a criterion: although the unions between "Blacks" and "Whites" produced fertile offspring, that fertility was supposed to dwindle as generations went by (hence the bizarre genealogy that links the term *mula* [mule] and *mulato*). The question of whether humans were one or several species (and, therefore, the importance of hybridism) was for a long time answered by the notion of the unity of the species—a thesis that the "race"/culture separation and the relativism of classical anthropology helped to establish.

Now that hybridism has again become an issue, one should note that it could be (and was) summoned to mean counterfusion and disjunction as much as fusion and assimilation (Young 1995: 18). Young outlines several standpoints in the early-twentieth-century discussions on hybridism: (1) The polygenist argument, denying that different peoples could mix, since the outcome would be infertile; (2) the amalgamation thesis, stating that all could cross, generating a new "race"; (3) the decomposition thesis, stating that mixed products die fast or revert to one of the two permanent types; (4) the argument that hybridism varies between close and distant species, being fertile among close "races" and infertile among distant ones; (5) the negative version of the amalgamation thesis, stating that miscegenation produces a mongrel group, a chaos without "race." Let us keep in mind these hypotheses, for I think that they come back, in analogical form, in the debates on cultural hybridism.

According to Young, notions about "races" and their mixture revolve around an ambivalent axis of desire and aversion: a structure of attraction, in which peoples and cultures mix and fuse, thus transforming themselves; and a structure of aversion, in which the different elements remain distinct and are dialogically opposed. The notion of "race" only works when it is defined in opposition to potential mixing. Ann Laura Stoler (1997), for instance, examined how the colonial authorities and the racial distinctions were structured fundamentally in terms of gender. The very categories of colonizer and colonized were maintained by forms of sexual control. Inclusion or exclusion ultimately demanded the regulation of the sexual, conjugal, and domestic lives of colonizers and colonized. That is probably why, according to her, in the early twentieth century concubinage was denounced for mining precisely that which decades before it was thought to consolidate. Local women, who had previously been seen as protectors of the men's well being, were portrayed as bearers of sinister diseases and influences.

These developments established some recurring patterns: colonial sexual prohibitions were racially asymmetrical and gender specific; the interdictions of interracial unions seldom were a primary impulse in strategies of domination; interracial unions (not so marriage) between European men and colonized women helped the long-term settling of men, at the same time that they guaranteed that property remained in the hands of a few. "Mixture" was systematically tolerated and even supported in the early colonial times (in India, Indochina, and South Africa). Miscegenation was neither a sign of absence nor presence of racial prejudice. The hierarchies of privilege and power were inscribed in the support or condemnation of interracial unions (Stoler 1997: 336). Miscegenation per se does not have a social meaning: one needs to inquire as to the type of miscegenation, how it occurred, between whom it occurred, and so on, before embarking on any positive (or negative) value judgment.

Transposing hybridism onto the cultural arena, it is common today to accept the idea—systematically presented by Stuart Hall (1992)—that modern nations are all cultural hybrids. Some of the new identities revolve around "tradition" while others accept impurity, turning around what Bhabha calls "translation," that is, formations of identity that cross borders and include people who have been dispersed from their homeland. These people supposedly negotiate with the new cultures they encounter, but are not assimilated. They will never, however, unify in the old sense—they are hybrid cultures, lived by people who are irrevocably *translated*. The hybridism resulting from postcolonial diasporas would have its reverse in the new nationalisms/fundamentalisms (the two being part of the same system). Hall uses the example of the shift in Black cultural politics. At first the term *Black* referred to the common experience of marginalization, thus denoting a politics of resistance. Today it is superimposed by a politics of representation that includes the notion of Black experience as an experience of diaspora. Is it possible, then, to say that hybridism takes for granted (as was the case with nineteenth-century racial theories) the previous existence of pure, fixed, and separate antecedents? Young proposes a tentative answer:

> The question is whether the old essentializing categories of cultural identity, or of race, were really so essentialized, or have been retrospectively constructed as more fixed than they were ... Today it is common to claim that we have moved from biologism and scientism to the safety of culturalism, safety in the critique of essentialism: but that shift has not been so absolute, for the racial was always cultural, the essential never unequivocal ... Culture and race developed together, imbricated within each other. (1995: 27)

In fact, we have been witnessing a public censoring of the notion of "race": the term has gone underground under the cloak of "culture" (see Stolcke 1995). Instead of a simpler situation, we find ourselves in a more complicated one.

A Short Tropical Note

One of the classical locations for discussions of hybridism and *miscigenação* or *mestiçagem* (and its relation to the idea of nation) is Latin America, especially the nations with a strong presence of descendants of Africans. Peter Wade (1993) has conducted one of the best analyses of the interaction between discrimination and *mestiçagem* (*mestizaje* in the Hispanic case). This interaction between patterns of discrimination and tolerance happens within the identity project of the national elites, who set forth the notion of an essentially mixed—*mestiza*—nation. Although it is generally accepted that "races" are social constructions or categorical identifications based on a discourse on the physical aspect and ancestry, Wade notes, however, that that which passes for physical difference and ancestry is not at all obvious. Apparently there is a "natural fact" of phenotypic variation on the basis of which culture constructs categorical identifications. But the act of defining a nature/culture relation mediated by this productionistic logic (Haraway 1989: 13) obscures the fact that there is no such thing as a prediscursive and universal encounter with "nature" and, therefore, with phenotypic variation (Wade 1993: 3). Therefore, racial categories are doubly processual: first, as a result of the variable perceptions of the nature/culture division that they mediate; second, as a result of the play between claims and attributions of identity in the context of relations of power (Wade 1993: 4).

The emergence of nationalism in Latin America did not involve the national incorporation of the lower classes in the European fashion. It was mediated by

Creole elites (in the Hispanic sense: Europeans born in the Americas) who had been excluded from political control during the colonial period (Anderson 1983: 50). One central problem was the contradiction between the mixed nature of the population and the "white" connotations of progress and modernity. The problem was "solved" with a compromise: to celebrate *mestizaje* as the core of Latin American originality. On the other hand, Blacks and Indians were romanticized as part of a glorious past and it was foreseen that they would be integrated in the future—in a process that would involve further racial mixing, preferably with whitening consequences (Wade 1993: 10). This compromise is obvious in the way racial theories of the time were received. They tended to classify Blacks and Indians as inferior, and hybrids were thought to be negatively influenced by these "races." But the elites tended to downplay the negative implications by minimizing biological determinism, emphasizing instead environmental and educational factors (as did, for instance, Gilberto Freyre in Brazil, with the use of neo-Lamarckianism). However, underneath the democratic discourse on *mestiçagem* and *mestizaje* lay the hierarchical discourse on whitening.

In Brazil, and according to Seyferth (1991), both those who supported whitening and those who were against African or Asian immigration (as well as those who privileged European immigration) believed that the Brazilian people or "race" needed yet to be formed through a melting pot process that would result in homogeneity. But they all imagined European immigrants as representatives of superior "races" destined to whiten a *mestiço* and Black population. Paradoxically, the latter were supposed to "Brazilianize" the European immigrants (Seyferth 1991: 179). The belief that Brazil has no racial question because there is no prejudice—a common feature in both everyday and social science theories—has paradoxically served to legitimize the emphasis in the miscegenation of "races" seen as unequal—thus presupposing the "triumph" (genetic but also civilizational) of the White "race."

First Period: "An Unfortunate Experiment of the Portuguese"

I would like to focus on the Portuguese case, while keeping in mind the Brazilian one, since Brazil has been an object of transfer and projection in the construction of Portuguese national representations. Once Brazil became independent, the focus of Portuguese governments shifted direction toward the African colonies. The new colonization of Africa was slow and did not amount to much in the way of practical results (see Alexandre & Dias 1998). But the notion of empire and the national utopia of building "New Brazils" were part of the boosting and maintenance of national pride. Nevertheless, academic and elite discourses, such as anthropology, focused mainly on the definition of Portugal and the Portuguese. A consistent and lasting colonial anthropology was practically nonexistent. This does not, however, preclude that self-representations were also based on representations of the colonial Other, even if there was no miscegenation with those Others. Miscegenation had been useful in the construction of Brazil as a neo-European nation in the Americas, but would be contradictory with a notion of Empire in Africa.

We can identify three "periods" in the debates on hybridism and miscegenation. Both Tamagnini and Mendes Correia can personify the first period, which was one of concern with the racial definition of the Portuguese and of opposition to miscegenation. A second, more culturalist period is personified by Jorge Dias and the influence of Freyre in his work; it is a period of concern with the plural ethnic origins of the Portuguese and with the resolution of the "colonial problem" in the light of the Brazilian experience. Finally, a third period would correspond to the post-1974 era and can only be outlined in terms of the contemporary multiculturalist debates.

Eusébio Tamagnini and Mendes Correia were the leaders of the two schools of anthropology in Coimbra and Oporto, respectively. Their work influenced a period that encompasses the constitutional monarchy, the First Republic, and the dictatorship of the *Estado Novo*. I will focus mainly on Tamagnini.[4] In 1902, in a paper on the population of São Tomé, composed of early settlers and indentured labor migration, Tamagnini asked: "The crossing between colonizing and colonized races: what is the worth of its products?" (1902: 11, *in* Santos 1996: 43). His answer was: "… the dialect of São Tomé, being a Creole that belongs to the second group, must be seen as a degenerate version of Continental Portuguese" (1902: 13 *in* Santos 1996: 43). Further on he says that

> … Easiness in relationships among the natives resulted necessarily in unfaithfulness and jealousy, which are obviously the causes for most crimes committed in Creole societies: prostitution, indecent behavior, and its repugnant varieties, such as pederasty, lesbianism, rape, and so on, which are practiced in a terrifying way in Creole societies, and which are the most obvious evidence of the shameful way in which the European peoples have been civilizing and colonizing the other peoples that they call savages. (1902: 39–40 in Santos 1996: 49)

Language, gender, sexuality, national identity, and colonialism: Robert Young could have based his work on Tamagnini alone. Besides being an indication of how the concept of gender was conceived as analogous to that of "race" (see Stepan 1986 and the first section of this chapter)—in a process in which scientists used racial difference to explain gender difference and vice versa—what we witness here is also a moral and political discourse on colonialism and its implication in the construction of national identity. Throughout his career, Tamagnini was to publish several studies from 1916 to 1949. Influenced by Broca's and Topinard's work, he was looking for anthropometric statistical averages of the Portuguese and their coincidence with those of the Europeans. In 1936 he concluded that "we can define the studied population thus: dolichocephalic, … of medium height, with brownish or pale white skin, brown or black hair, dark eyes" (Tamagnini

1936: 195 in Santos 1996: 108). Therefore, he concludes, "the Portuguese can … be considered members of the Mediterranean race" (Tamagnini 1936: 195, in Santos 1996: 108). Nor did the nasal index of the Portuguese "reveal any quantitatively relevant sign of *mestiçagem* with platirhine Negroid elements" (1944: 22, in Santos 1996: 114–115).

Although after the 1920s he had to take into consideration the developments in genetics, he did so within a Malthusian framework in connection with colonial issues. In the First National Congress of Colonial Anthropology in 1934 in Oporto (one year after the legislation of the Colonial Act), he warned of the dangers of *mestiçagem*: "When two peoples or two races have reached different cultural levels and have organized completely different social systems, the consequences of *mestiçagem* are necessarily disastrous" (Tamagnini 1934a: 26 in Santos 1996: 137). In a panel on population in the 1940 Congress on the Portuguese World (at the occasion of the Portuguese World Expo), he presented a study about the blood groups of the Portuguese and concluded that the Portuguese population had "been able to maintain relative ethnic purity and although the origins in a Nordic type have to be found within the mutations in a brown dolichocephalous past, we, the Portuguese, as representatives of that common ancestor cannot be accused of having spoiled [literally 'made bastards of'] the family" (Tamagnini 1940: 22 in Santos 1996: 145). However, in 1944 he had to acknowledge—albeit with one important safeguard—that:

> …It would be foolish to pretend denying the existence of *mestiçagem* between the Portuguese and the elements of the so-called colored races. The fact that they are a colonizing people makes it impossible to avoid ethnic contamination. What one can not accept is the raising of such *mestiçagem* to the category of a sufficient factor of ethnic degeneration to such a point that anthropologists would have to place the Portuguese outside the white races or classify them as Negroid *mestiços* … (Tamagnini 1944 in Santos 1996: 12)

One year before his appointment as Minister of Education (he held the post from 1934 to 1936), he suggested the creation of a Society of Eugenic Studies. In 1938 psychiatrist Barahona Fernandes was supporting eugenics against the "false behaviorist idea" (influenced by Lamarck's transformationism) of the human being as a reflection of the environment (Pimentel 1998: 18). In the year following the 1926 coup that established dictatorship, Mendes Correia (head of the Institute of Anthropology and Ethnology in Oporto)[5] had called for the segregation of relapsing criminals, the sterilization of degenerates, the regulation of immigration, and the banning of marriage for professional beggars. In 1932 Mendes Correia invited Renato Kehl, president of the Brazilian Eugenics Organization, to give a lecture in Oporto. On the occasion, the Brazilian scientist proposed the introduction of both positive and negative eugenic measures, publicized the advantages of marriage within the same class or race, and condemned *mestiçagem* for being "dissolving, dissuasive, demoralizing, and degrading" (Pimentel 1998: 18).

Although eugenics was not a successful approach in Portugal, the question of "racial improvement" was much discussed in 1934, in relation to the colonial question and the issue of *mestiçagem*. Although some participants in the First Congress of Colonial Anthropology praised *mestiçagem*, Tamagnini was against it. Based on a study of somatology and aptitude tests done with sixteen Cape Verdean and six Macanese *mestiços* who had come to the Colonial Expo of 1934 in Oporto, Mendes Correia concluded that miscegenation was a condemnable practice. In the plenary session Tamagnini recalled that "the little repugnance that the Portuguese have regarding sexual approaches to elements of other ethnic origins is often presented as evidence of their higher colonizing capacity," and asserted that "it is necessary to change radically such an attitude" (Tamagnini 1934b: 26 in Castelo 1998: 111). He continues: "It is in the social arena that the fact of *mestiçagem* has graver consequences. The *mestiços*, because they do not adapt to either system, are rejected by both …" (in Castelo 1998: 111). Mendes Correia couldn't agree more: "being mulatto is longing for oneself [*o mulato é Saudade de si mesmo*] … just like the despised hermaphrodite outcries the conflict between the sexes … the *mestiço* is thus an unexpected being in the plan of the world, an unfortunate experiment of the Portuguese" (Mendes Correia 1940: 122 in Castelo 1998: 112).

Also in the Congress on the Portuguese World, ethnographer Pires de Lima countered Gilberto Freyre's thesis on the hybrid origin of the Portuguese. Lima said that there had only been three fundamental ethnic groups: Lusitanians, Romans, and Germanics. He saw Jews, Moors and Blacks as "intruders" (Castelo 1998: 114), and he strongly objected to the promotion of miscegenation. His ideas could not be more in agreement with the representations of the national identity sponsored by the *Estado Novo* and they are still present today in the public's mind, that is, the collective amnesia regarding those three peoples who were either expelled or "whitened."

Second Period: The Luso-Tropical Fever

Gilberto Freyre's theses were to be adopted by Jorge Dias, the renovator of Portuguese anthropology after Mendes Correia (Dias's predecessor at the Oporto school).[6] For Dias, the unity of the Portuguese is the outcome of a melting pot of different ethnic origins. Colonial situations, on the other hand, must be distinguished: the Brazilian and the Cape Verdean contexts, on the one hand, are based on miscegenation; and the continental African contexts, on the other, are marked by weak colonization and a late White migration (after 1940 only). Dias showed his opposition to Tamagnini and Mendes Correia. In 1956 he said that the creation of the *mestiço* is positive for the human genetic pool and that he believed that the Luso-Tropical *mestiço* was the man of the future (Castelo 1998: 120).

In the late 1950s and early 1960s, the legitimization (or the contestation) of colonialism could no longer be done with arguments of political-economic interest and sovereignty claims, but increasingly with "socio-anthropological" arguments, even when marked by a strong mythical character. According to Cláudia Castelo, the reception of Gilberto Freyre's work was not uniform in Portugal. Right-wing intellectuals made a nationalistic interpretation of it, reducing Freyre's ideas to appraisal of Portuguese colonial exceptionalism. Those on the left were more critical and tended to compare the doctrine with the historical facts and political practice. The project of imperial renaissance had been, up until then, on the antipodes of Freyre's ideas. Many supporters of the dictatorial regime assumed that the Black "race" was inferior and were against *mestiçagem*. Not until after World War II—with the rechristening of the colonies as "overseas provinces" and the abolishment of the Colonial Act—did the notion of a pluriracial and pluricontinental nation come close to Freyre's interpretation. Freyre's famous journey to the Portuguese colonies started two months after the 1951 constitutional amendments that abolished the Act. Freyre's account of his journeys enabled the first in a series of appropriations of his ideas by the Portuguese government for purposes of international propaganda. Luso-Tropicalist doctrine soon became Portugal's weapon against the international pressures for decolonialization.

Political scientist Adriano Moreira fully incorporated the doctrine into his analyses and political projects after the 1950s. It was not until the 1960s, once the colonial wars had started, that he (as Overseas Minister, from 1960 to 1962) tried to narrow the gap between theory and practice. The Native Status Laws were abolished (they separated citizens from natives and prescribed forced labor) and relative autonomy was granted to colonial governments. But Moreira was to be ousted from power by the "integrationist" sectors of the regime. His version of "multiracialism" nonetheless became a staple in the regime's colonial and nationalistic vocabulary. In 1961 he had written: " … we want to make it clear to the commonwealth of nations that it is our nation's resolve to pursue a policy of multiracial integration, without which there will be neither peace nor civilization in Black Africa … a policy whose benefits are illustrated by the largest country of the future that is Brazil …" (Moreira 1961: 10–11).

The regime's propaganda stated that Portuguese Africa would one day be like Brazil, that is, a "racial democracy." Consequently, he had to explain that the Native Status Laws had been misunderstood, saying that it was "just because of our concern with authenticity that our … Native Status Laws deny the natives the political rights related to such institutions [of sovereignty; he is referring to the right to vote, among others], many accused us of denying them nationality [citizenship]" (1961: 12).[7] Moreira uses, then, the argument of authenticity and preservation of ethnic particularism as justification. To different cultures (and "races") accrue different rights, in order to respect identities—that seems to be the rationale. This sort of "right-wing multiculturalism" remains alive today in many sectors. That is why a more liberal and emancipatory multiculturalism can only be successful if cultural essentialism and particularism are put aside.

"Assimilation" was a central concept in the colonial administration. It was often juxtaposed to Freyre's and Dias's notions of *miscibilidade*. These are common themes in the historiography of Portuguese expansion, the Discoveries, and colonialism, as well as in the so-called "sociology of the formation of Brazil" (of which Freyre's work is an example), and also in the wider debates on Portuguese national identity and ethnogenesis. Moreira said that "cultures, not races, can be eternal" (1958: 20). It is on the basis of this presupposition that he was in favor of interracial marriages, allegedly because the family was the best instrument for the creation of multiracial societies. Nevertheless, he said that miscegenation could cause a problem: "we have fewer mixed families today than in the past ... because the deficit of white women has diminished. *Mestiços* now tend to close up as a group, which is not beneficial for integration" (Moreira 1958: 154). The source of concern is clear: in the colonial context of Portuguese Africa, a *mestiço* group could become a specific social and professional group, tied to the administrative hierarchy, living in the cities, playing the role of mediators and thus potentially generating nationalist and anticolonial feelings. The ambiguous discourse on miscegenation in the late colonial period was, therefore, the very negation of hybridism.

Freyre's influence is a fascinating case. If, in Brazil, his ideas can be interpreted as either left wing or right wing depending on context, in Portugal the dictatorial and colonial atmosphere increased their ambiguity. Freyre's ideas can undoubtedly be appropriated as humanistic and antiracist; the problem lies in the veracity of his argument about Portuguese colonization, allowing for political arguments that underplay racist practices because of the expected utopia of full miscegenation, Brazilian style (which is, anyway, a mystification of the Brazilian racial formation). I have said in the previous chapter that I believe that Freyre condensed a diffuse argument—somewhere between common sense and hegemony—that links the theories of national identity and formation in both Brazil and Portugal (as well as the modern Portuguese colonial project in Africa). It is a mythical discourse with scientific pretensions. Freyre's argument focuses on the supposed disposition of the Portuguese to engage in "hybrid and slave-based" colonization of the tropical lands. This disposition is supposedly explained by the Portuguese ethnic and cultural past as an "undefined" people (1933: 5). This lack of definition (i.e., "racial" and cultural purity) amounts to a "balance of antagonisms" (1933: 6), and Portuguese "plasticity," based on *aclimatibilidade, mobilidade e miscibilidade* (adaptation to different climates, mobility, and the ability to mingle/miscegenate), was the strategy for compensating demographic weakness, thus building a colonial system based on the patriarchal and slave-owning family.

Freyre's narrative occupied center stage in the construction of Brazilian self-representations. But it is a development of discourses on Portuguese exceptionalism that are prior to Freyre's; and which were made systematic, as doctrine, after his intellectual output and in the context of colonialism in Africa.

The central problem is that interpretations of Brazilian and Portuguese ethnogenesis were both done through a positive reinterpretation of historical processes of extreme inequality, thanks to the neutral presentation of the notion of miscegenation, forcefully separated from racialized social and economic relations. This became a central problem in the national definitions in both countries, among the Black movement in Brazil, and in the identity redefinitions in postcolonial Portugal.

In Portugal, Jorge Dias dealt with the set of psychological qualities that supposedly defined the specificity of Portuguese culture. Geographical conditions and miscegenation hold a primary place in his theory. It also focuses on the "expansionistic character" and in "plasticity." However, before he was to write on ethnic psychology in the American Culture and Personality sense, Dias made a point of closing the debate on the Lusitanians, which had been paramount in the nineteenth century. Then, anthropologists, historians, and archaeologists concerned with finding the Portuguese originality had constructed the Lusitanians as the ancestors of the Portuguese. Jorge Dias presented an alternative ethnogenealogy, in which pluralism became the explanatory factor for Portuguese singularity (although, of course, the notion of originality remained, instead of the assumption that all peoples have plural ethnic genealogies). João Leal says that this narrative allowed for the construction of a gallery of ethnic ancestors more in tune with the sort of diffusionism that had influenced Dias (Leal 200b). But it allowed most for the supposed originality of Portugal: the unique capacity for mixing cultures.

Third Period: National Identity and "New Cultural Classes"

Fifty years of dictatorship, colonial wars until the 1970s, and the tutelage of the Brazilian myth have marked heavily the self-representations of the Portuguese in the democratic and postcolonial period. In 1974 democracy was reestablished, and in the following two years the colonies became independent. In 1986 Portugal joined the European Union, and this golden period closed with the commemorations of the five hundredth anniversary of the Discoveries and the opening of Expo 98. It was in the 1980s that a public debate on "racism" started in Portugal, as well as the antiracist movement and the cultural salience of the growing African migrant communities, mainly in Lisbon.

The Luso-Tropicalist discourse has long been an everyday theory and an integral part of Portuguese representations of nationality. It is a dense and pervasive discourse because it contains the very promises that progressive politics could subscribe to, namely the notion of miscegenation and hybridization, provided that unequal power relations are elided. The effect of racial hegemony that Hanchard (1994) reports for Brazil (culturalism as a factor that precludes ethnopolitical mobilization) works similarly in Portugal. But it is strengthened here by the historical amnesia about some ethnogenetic contributions (Jews,

Africans, Arabs), slavery, colonialism, and the colonial wars. These issues are now being raised in Portuguese society at the same time that a redefinition of national identity vis-à-vis the European Union is being done. Notions related to the Portuguese diaspora and "Lusophony" are also being invented. Jorge Vala et al. (1999), in a study on racism in Portugal, say that

> It is common to think that the specificity of our culture and of our colonial history, the easy miscegenation of the Portuguese with other peoples, the fact that many Blacks residing in Portugal are national citizens, or the fact that most African immigrants come from the former colonies have all contributed to the specificity of a possible sort of racism in Portugal. In the end, this idea is still a consequence of the "Luso-Tropicalist" ideology, and political actors from different areas sponsor it. However, the results of our study demonstrate that racist social beliefs in Portugal are organized in ways similar to other European countries, that the factors are not significantly different from those underlying subtle or flagrant racism in other countries, and that in Portugal, as in other European countries, the antiracist norm applies to flagrant racism, not to subtle racism ... (Vala et al. 1999: 194)

As a matter of fact, at the same time that there is public censorship of flagrant racism (allowing for the reproduction of the subtle kind), a paradoxical process is happening. Teresa Fradique, in her study on rap says that it is " ... [the definition of] a product through the outlining of its difference (cultural, social, racial) vis-à-vis the society in which it emerges; it is then presented as a national product ..." (Fradique 1998: 110). I have observed a similar process going on in Brazil, in my study of the Black movement and the politics of cultural representation. Fradique, after defining an association between ethnic group, social inequality, and culture, sees ethnic minorities as "a kind of 'new cultural class,' made homogeneous due precisely to a fuzzy mixing of those three categories, and politically and sociologically created in order to manage the new configurations which are inherent to postcolonial societies" (1998: 123). This process, which involves an antiracist discourse that objectifies cultures, is similar to new racisms, not only in Stolcke's terms (culture instead of race), but also in Gilroy's: the capacity to associate discourses on patriotism, nationalism, xenophobia, militarism, and sexual difference in a complex system that gives race its contemporary meaning, constituted around two central concepts: identity and culture (Gilroy 1987: 43).

Parallel to this, multiculturalism has been one of the rhetorical devices most used by the politics of identity (Comaroff 1996; Hobsbawm 1996) in postcolonial contexts. The dominant ideas in multiculturalism always presuppose an authoritative center of cultural reference, which ends up functioning with the logic of assimilation. Its main keywords are tolerance and integration. Vertovec (1996) points to the correspondence between multicultural initiatives and some arguments of the new cultural racisms. Both use culturalist perspectives: the multicultural society is divided into several unicultural subunits, and culture is seen as a human characteristic that is virtually embedded in the genes of individuals (1996: 51; see Stolcke 1995). Segal and Handler talk of a culturalization of races, in which difference is objectified in an ensemble of multiple singular cultures (1995: 391–399).

Issues such as Luso-Tropical specificity, historical miscegenation, racial democracy, or the nonracism of the Portuguese and the Brazilians have been faced in diverse ways: as ideologies that mask a harsher reality; as an outcome of racial hegemony; as a form of naïve wishful thinking, compensating for the structural weaknesses of both countries; or as having some validity and an unaccomplished potential that can become a political project for the future. Miscegenation, *mestiçagem,* and hybridism remain discursive knots that contaminate emancipatory practices with ambiguity.[8]

In a 1997 article, Angela Gilliam calls attention to Peter Fry's critique of Hanchard. Fry claims that the multiple mode of racial classification in Brazil allows individuals to be classified in varied ways, thus deracializing individual identity. The Black movement's contestation of this model supposedly led to the denial of any sort of Brazilian specificity. The bipolar mode—typical of the United States and the Black militants—endorses the racist notion of the One Drop Rule (Fry 1995–1996)[9]. Gilliam, however, says that Blacks themselves have changed the One Drop Rule, from the concept of pollution to that of inclusion (1997: 89). Sansone, who supports Fry, accuses certain researchers of "Lusophobia," scholars (especially Skidmore 1994) whose major concern seems to be to criticize the "ambiguity" of Brazilian racial relations and who are fascinated by a hypothetical bipolarization (Sansone 1996: 215). Hanchard classifies Fry and Sansone as neo-Freyrians, since the multipolar model supports Freyre's view that miscegenation and hybridism would lead to the democratization of racial relations (Hanchard 1997). However, he says, multipolar analysis does not confront the miscegenation factor, and the role of the Black woman in the formation of national culture is not acknowledged in any place in the multipolar ambiguity.

Gilliam agrees, saying that the extension of the narrative of *mestiçagem* to the twentieth century annihilates the chances of power and authority of women over their lives and elides the predatory sexuality that has affected the lives of Indian and Black women (1997: 93). Acknowledging that neither model is problem free, she appeals to Gilroy, who would say that Blacks are caught between both. Gilroy rejects even creolization and other theories on Caribbean identity—*métissage, mestizaje* and hybridism—since they all are as inadequate as the Manichean dynamics of Black and White in the definition of Black identity (Balutansky 1997: 242 in Gilliam 1997: 93). It is therefore hard to deny Blacks the manipulation of hypodescent, and one must show how false the notion is that racial mixture means absence of racism.

In Portugal, while the production of Black cultural specificities is arising, and while subtle racism persists under the condemnation of flagrant racism, two factors are occurring: on the one hand (and I shall not deal with it in depth here) the way that discourses about commemoration (Discoveries, Expo, etc.) are permeated by the rhetoric of multiculturalism, tolerance, and culture contact, and the other, a redefinition of nationality. Schiller and Fouron (1997) say that the political leaders of countries such as Portugal have been redefining their respective nation-states as transnational ones so as to include their populations in the diaspora. The authors claim that underlying this are concepts of national identity marked by the issue of "race," presupposing a line of descent and blood ties. States that export emigrants define nationality along the line of descent, not through the shared language, history, culture or territory.

This raises a problem: Lusophony—for instance—as a global geostrategic concept would serve to define "culture." Culture would be something given to others by Portugal. Nationality, however, would be only for those who belong in the genealogy. In this sense miscegenation and *mestiçagem* are discursively constructed as the passing of Portuguese blood to the others—in the past—and rarely the other way around. And when the others are among us, the definition of their cultural authenticity places them outside nationality, although they are allowed to enjoy multiculturalism.

Schiller and Fouron (1997) show how European nations in the late nineteenth century considered national history according to specific lineages—the Arians, the Celts, and so on. The same happened in Portugal with the debate on the Lusitanians (see Leal 2000b). But the semiperipheral specificity of Portugal, her empire, and post-Brazilian colonialism in Africa led to an accentuation of the notion of *mestiçagem*, although the abolition of contrary laws came late, with the end of the Native Status Laws. Referring to Wade (1993), Schiller and Fouron say that even when miscegenation is exalted, it is often implicitly defined as in opposition to the color Black, and the latter is not mentioned or acknowledged in the narrative of racial mixture. The language of the color White is the one adopted even when the nation defines itself as a product of miscegenation. This process went further in Portugal, since it is not a neo-European nation in the Americas, but a colonizing center (albeit a weak and semiperipheral one).

Afterword

It is no longer a question of "measuring" whether miscegenation is good or bad for the future of the "races." It is no longer a question of discussing the difference between "race" and "culture." It is no longer a question of evaluating those debates in terms of the construction or maintenance of either nation-states or colonial empires. Nowadays the terms describing situations of hybridism in postcolonial contexts and increasing globalization present them as accomplished facts or as expressions of political correctness or wishful thinking. The present discourse on hybridism seems to be challenged by emancipatory movements such as the Black movement, with its refusal of syncretism; by neonationalist movements that are eager for ethnic cleansing; and by deconstructionism and the criticism of postmodern anthropologists. While in the practices of social life people seem to go on reproducing a covert horror toward mixture—and social barriers that perpetuate "races" are reproduced—the praising of cultural mixture (one in which each contribution is clearly defined) emerges in the field of cultural consumption products. During a brief visit to Portugal, Bahian Black musician Carlinhos Brown said:

> This is an album and a show that celebrates miscegenation in Brazil ... that remixing is a feeling that only the miscegenated knows. It is like having loved a woman for the first time: the orgasm is different ... The miscegenated one is ... the man of the third millennium ... and in the end of the millennium there is no people like the Portuguese people who can rightfully celebrate. I do not know if Portugal is aware of that. Because Portugal conquered miscegenation: to unite peoples through the easiest way, through taste, through sight, through acceptance. Portugal may have been a great good for the Black culture. (*Público*, 5 August 1999, page 21)

This is, of course, more than wishful thinking—it is the reproduction of ideology, and an effect of hegemony. But it also indicates a utopian aspiration, albeit a misplaced one. Hybridism, miscegenation, and correlate terms have a tense history behind them. Any cultural, social, or political project that intends to promote *mixture* for the promotion of *new* social realities will necessarily also have to be a critical project, one that evaluates and learns from that tense history of practices and knowledges. Anthropologists could contribute to this with the critical and comparative analysis of those social formations, namely the so-called Creole ones, which *may* constitute a glimpse of the desired future, even if they are the by-products of the conflict of the colonial encounter.

Notes

1. I use the Portuguese expression instead of the better-known Spanish *mestizaje*, which I see as more specific to Hispanic South America than is acknowledged by its use in the literature in English.
2. My translation, and throughout the chapter.
3. In this case I have kept the original Portuguese expressions. Most are slang terms for several "phenotypic" classifications from Brazil and Portuguese-speaking Africa.
4. References to Tamagnini were taken from Santos (1996). Since these are indirect references, I list them here, not in the final list of references: E. Tamagnini, 1902, *Dissertação para a Cadeira de Antropologia e Arqueologia Pré-Histórica*, Coimbra, FCUC; 1904, *Psychologia Feminina*, Coimbra, IAUC; 1934a, "Lição inaugural do ano lectivo de 1934–35," *Revista da Faculdade de Ciências da Universidade de Coimbra*, 5; 1934b, "Problemas de mestiçagem," Oporto, Edições da Primeira Exposição Colonial Portuguesa; 1936b, "A pigmentação dos portugueses," *Contribuições para o Estudo da Antropologia Portuguesa*, 1 (3), Coimbra, IAUC; 1940, "Os grupos sanguíneos dos portugueses," *Revista da Faculdade de Ciências da Universidade de Coimbra*, 8; 1944b, "O índice nasal dos portugueses," *Contribuições para o Estudo da Antropologia Portuguesa*, 5 (1), Coimbra, IAUC.
5. He was also the mayor of Oporto from 1936 to 1942, a member of the Chamber of Corporations (a Corporativist assembly in the *Estado Novo*) in 1945, and the director of the Colonial School for a period.

6. Although he later published several books and papers on the specific theme of Luso-Tropicalism, his theses are already implicit in his seminal work on the formation of Brazil, *Casa Grande e Senzala: Formação da Família Brasileira sob o Regime da Economia Patriarcal* (Vol. 1 of *Introdução à História da Sociedade Patriarcal no Brasil*), first published in 1933. First English edition: 1946, *The Masters and the Slaves (A Study on the Development of Brazilian Civilization)*, New York: Knopf. Jorge Dias's theses are explained in several publications. The following were used for the present paper: 1968, "O carácter nacional português na presente conjuntura," *Boletim da Academia Internacional da Cultura Portuguesa*, 4; 1971, "Estudos do Carácter Nacional Português," *Estudos de Antropologia Cultural*, 7, Lisbon: JIU; 1950, "Os elementos fundamentais da cultura portuguesa," *Estudos de Antropologia*, vol I, Lisbon: INCM; 1956, "Paralelismo no processo da formação das nações," *Estudos de Antropologia*, vol. 1, Lisbon: INCM.

7. The population of the Portuguese colonies in Africa was divided into three legal status groups: colonials/nationals, assimilated, and natives. This form of classification, contrary in essence to miscegenation, did not apply in those territories where "local civilization" was acknowledged (for instance, India) or that were the result of "hybrid" colonization (White colonials and Black slaves in unpopulated land), such as Cape Verde.

8. João Pina-Cabral, in an analysis of the different meanings of racism for the man on the street and anthropologists, suggests a third way, beyond the neo-Freyrian vs. anti-Freyrian divide: "I do not refute Charles Boxer's contention that there was discrimination, prejudice and ethnic violence in the Portuguese colonial empire, like certain hasty nationalists are again denying. It is just that we cannot deny the evidence of the fact that interethnic barriers based on color were not constructed and maintained in the same way in the British and Portuguese colonial empires" (Pina-Cabral 1998: 20, my translation). I subscribe to this position because, otherwise, the perceptions of color differences by common people in Portugal would have to be dismissed by the anthropologists as "false consciousness," and because denying *exceptionalism* is not tantamount to denying *specificity*.

9. North American folk theory according to which one is "Black" if one has at least one "Black" ancestor, no matter how remote, and even when phenotypic "evidence" counters the classification.

5

Epilogue of Empire: East Timor and the Portuguese Postcolonial Catharsis

Introduction

On 30 August 1999, East Timorese cast their ballots in a referendum that took place under the auspices of the UN and was based on a signed agreement between Portugal and Indonesia.[1] At stake was the acceptance or rejection of a proposal for special autonomy within Indonesia, which if rejected would surely result in real independence for East Timor. On 4 September, in simultaneous televised appearances the secretary general of the UN, Kofi Annan, and the head of UNAMET (UN Assistance Mission in East Timor) in Dili announced the results of what they considered to be a legitimate voting exercise: approximately 21 percent in favor and 79 percent against. The following day the Indonesian army and the pro–Indonesian integration militia began a systematic destruction of East Timorese territory. Part of the population fled to the mountains, others to voluntary or forced refuge in West Timor, while still others were killed outright. This situation speared a civic movement in Portugal of a proportion unseen since the revolutionary activities of 1974–75, subsequent to the fall of the Portuguese dictatorship.[2] The movement had an explicit objective: to force the Security Council of the UN, and especially the United States, to intervene in East Timor so as to guarantee the results of the referendum and to put an end to violence. The characteristics of the Portuguese movement to support East Timor—from the point of view of its implicit context and its process—make it an exceptional case for reflecting on the Portuguese postcolonial moment.

An Ethnographic Report of the Events

What happened in Portugal in September 1999? We can analyze the first events of the movement through a form of ethnographic reportage. By this I mean a description of events that is marked by my participation in them as a citizen, without the conscious purpose of using ethnographic methodology or initiating a research project. This is the reason why this chapter should be seen neither as an academic paper nor as an experimental text, but rather as an essay written by an anthropologist who pays attention to the politics of representation in his own society. When the pro–integration terror began in East Timor I immediately felt the same revulsion and indignation as millions of other citizens. The first reading was obvious: how was it possible not to accept the results of a referendum (sanctioned by the international community) in which the East Timorese had so unequivocally opted for independence? Democratic legitimacy was put on the line, and this in relation to what was seen, in Portugal, as a poor, illiterate, and suffering people: the moral superiority of democracy was thrown in our—we, its Western inventors—faces by those we had judged so many times as incapable of even understanding it. Moreover, I felt repulsed by the violence that was used by the occupation army and by the militias. Finally, I was surprised at myself because I had always been cautious in my support for the "Timorese cause," because it seemed (in Portugal and for its protagonists) to smack of colonial nostalgia.

The first event that I remember—that solidified my support for the civic movement—was the "three minutes of silence" on 8 September 1999, an initiative that was called for by several organizations and announced on the radio stations. I went outside a few minutes before the set time expecting nothing to happen. But my skepticism (and maybe even cynicism) were countered: at exactly three o'clock, in a neighborhood that was not central, and in which one would not expect a public performance of any significance, the traffic stopped and people got out of their cars. The stores around closed and people came out onto the sidewalk. Everyone was still. Someone shouted "Fascist!" to a car that did not stop. Above the skyline of buildings I noticed that traffic crossing the 25 de Abril Bridge had also halted. As I stood silent on the sidewalk, I remembered images I had seen of Holocaust Day in Israel where citizens do the very same thing. But above all, I felt a new emotion: I identified myself with all of the strangers around me who were doing what I was. "Communitas" was taking hold.[3]

The second episode was a human chain on the same day. A group of young people proposed that a human chain link the embassies of the permanent countries of the UN Security Council. I was still skeptical: The distance between the U.S. and French embassies is great and even more so with the detours necessary to link the Russian, British, and Chinese embassies. The total route was ten kilometers. As I lived near the French embassy, that is where I headed. To my amazement, the surrounding area was packed with people and the radios were announcing that not only was the chain complete but in many places it was two, three, four people thick. Later, television images taken by helicopter confirmed this.

The third episode that served to constitute the solidarity movement was the "dress in white" day. A radio station made an appeal that at least one white article of clothing be worn on that day or white banners be hung from the windows and that cars use a white ribbon. On the day, I dressed in a white pair of pants and shirt. I went out to the street and looked—as other passers-by did—to find that many had done the same. Not only was there a white streak of clothing visible on the street, there were also many windows draped with white sheets or bedspreads. Cars not only displayed white ribbons but also were decorated with little homemade-looking signs inscribed with ringing phrases like "Timor Lives," "Save Timor," and "Viva Timor Loro Sae" (Timor of the Rising Sun). In a building alongside the American embassy, long rolls of computer paper were hanging down out of windows.

A fourth episode, in which I did not participate, was a demonstration in Madrid on 12 September. As Portugal did not have diplomatic relations with Indonesia, the closest Indonesian embassy was in the Spanish capital. At the suggestion of the mayors of the region of the city of Oporto (Portugal's second-largest city), a demonstration was called for in front of the Indonesian embassy, buses were rented, and the railway company made a train available. Taking advantage of the freedom of circulation within the European Union, this demonstration took place, therefore, outside the national territory.

The fifth episode was the reception of Bishop Ximenes Belo on 10 September. The bishop of Dili (East Timor's capital) stopped in Lisbon on his way to the Vatican. The purpose of his visit was to celebrate Mass in the church of the congregation where he had studied, but the route from the airport to the church became the scene of a massive demonstration of welcome and concern. That this would be the case had been foreseen. The bishop traveled in an open car, accompanied by security guards and police who cleared the way. What had not been expected was the speed and spontaneity with which a human chain formed along the entire route. One minute the street was empty, the next it was full of people coming out from their homes, offices, or from stores and buses.

The same day the media announced that B. J. Habibie, the Indonesian president, had accepted the intervention of an international peacekeeping force in East Timor. The forces would start arriving in Dili on the eighteenth or nineteenth of the month. From that moment on the movement started to progressively dwindle until a few days before the Portuguese elections on 10 October 1999—immediately following the death of a national icon, Amália Rodrigues, the Fado singer. The subject of East Timor was then relegated once again to the back pages of the newspapers.[4]

Structure and Meaning of the Events

These manifestations had three recurring and overlapping aspects: organized gatherings and demonstrations, spontaneous performances, and the catalyzing role played by the media. The U.S. Embassy and the area around the delegation of the UN were rapidly established as the prime locations for demonstrations, gatherings, and spontaneous performance. Groups of demonstrators went back and forth between the two locations, whenever there was no demonstration that linked both. The location of the American embassy was evident but the location of the UN delegation was not so obvious. As it happens the delegation of the UN occupies a suite rented at the Sheraton Hotel—Lisbon's tallest building. Nothing on the exterior of the building signals its presence; it was never known which window the office lay behind, and no one ever appeared at that window. What I mean to say here is that the demonstrations took place in front of the "virtual" UN delegation headquarters, but in reality they took place in front of the Sheraton Hotel—a recognizable symbol of the globalization of American capitalism. Furthermore, the space in front of the hotel is far from a proper square, but rather a tangle of intersections. It doesn't have a name other than that given to it by demonstrators on improvised signs: Timor Loro Sae Square. The appropriation of urban space took place through an act of topological creation.[5]

From early on this "square" became the center of events. At any moment of the day there were people there, increasing in number as the afternoon turned to dusk. A pattern developed: the evenings began here and later moved to the American embassy. In front of the Sheraton, an encampment was established where some staged a hunger strike and others left their tokens of grief: posters, paintings on the ground, lit candles, and crosses. Out of this chaos on the sidewalk an authentic altar was created. Public figures and representatives of organized groups came by, even people like me who went knowing that they would meet someone they knew or a friend, ended up staying longer than they had planned, canceling appointments, and getting home late. On the adjacent avenue, drivers got in the habit of honking car horns. At certain moments groups of bikers would come by in noisy demonstrations. Suddenly, as if coming out of nowhere, small demonstrations would congregate in the square. In the opposite direction, groups leaving the square flooded into the avenue and fouled up the traffic, at which point drivers, rather than respond angrily, would explode with a supportive honking of horns. They would then disappear. Where to? No one knew.

Spontaneity and unpredictability became the dominant tone, perhaps only surpassed by the surprising social composition of the participants: people from the right and from the left, Catholics and nonreligious people, many more women than might be expected, and many children and youth. In addition, frequently it was the first time that many who were active had taken to the streets; many were participating in the first demonstrations of their lives. Even people in the habit of only going about town by car honked at the symbolic points in the city or wherever they might meet a demonstration in progress. The feeling that people had "taken to the streets" was accentuated by the fact that during these days, many people, including me, met acquaintances from long ago, high school friends not seen for some twenty years—and all expressing the same surprise at finding each other unexpectedly, out on the street.

The demonstrations included spontaneous performances, but these also took place in other contexts. Wearing the color white went on beyond the "dress in white" day. It became the color *de rigueur* for any event in which East Timor was the theme; hanging white banners in windows went on for many days; white lapel ribbons, emulating the red ones used to show support for the fight against AIDS, appeared; and cars sported the previously mentioned signs. The outlines of human bodies were traced on the ground at the locations where demonstrations took place. Candles were left burning and people offered themselves or their children as symbolic corpses to be outlined as if sacrificing and sanctifying them in the act. The tradition of mural painting, which had been dormant since 1976 (the year of "normalization," following the 1974–75 revolution), was also revived.

Around the country events multiplied: launching miniature sailboats in the rivers and sea, opening bank accounts to collect aid funds for humanitarian purposes and for the reconstruction of East Timor. Along with these events, the municipal government of Lisbon covered all the principal monuments of the city in black, altering the everyday aspect of the city with signs of mourning. The political powers thus allied themselves with the demonstrators.

The role of the mass media in the mobilization of the people reached unimagined proportions. One feature of this mobilization must be highlighted: the intensive focus on information regarding East Timor. This aspect raises two further questions: the role of the media in creating events and the way in which the media's interpretation of events in East Timor heightened Portuguese self-esteem (an experience common to practically the whole of the movement) in fueling the mobilization. The mobilization for East Timor was not stimulated by television, as much as one might have expected in a contemporary context. Rather, it was radio that played a more evocative role (by way of voice and language), proving the greater capacity of this medium to mobilize the listeners' imaginations. Radio, geared as it is to the urban context and the automobile, provided news and information more rapidly than television, spreading quickly via cars and transistor radios. The privately owned station TSF was transformed into a virtual political committee. The appeal for the "three minutes of silence" or the "dress in white" day was broadcast via TSF. Setting aside the news about other subjects and even canceling commercial spots, the station dedicated its broadcasts exclusively to the situation in East Timor and to the national mobilization in Portugal. An incantation was instituted that lasted until 10 October 1999: before the news and every half hour a voice announced: "It's ten o'clock in continental Portugal and in Madeira, an hour earlier in the Azores, and five p.m. in Dili." An everyday informative phrase thus became a statement. The ambiguity of this statement (including East Timor in Portugal, but doing so to express support for that country's struggle) encapsulates the ambiguity of the whole process, be it in the significance of civic mobilization or in the more general framework of the question of East Timor for the postcolonial reconfiguration of Portugal. The boundary between solidarity with East Timor and its inclusion in a transnational "Portugueseness" bordering on colonial nostalgia was never drawn. But this is a fundamental question to which I turn in the last part of this essay.

The mobilization also extended into media that had not been used on such a massive scale in Portugal before, particularly the Internet. There were many initiatives that circulated widely, including petitions during demonstrations, media appeals for the donation of funds and proposals from all sorts of organizations suggesting that a day's wages be turned over to support the struggle. However, the petitions promoting international solidarity that circulated by way of the Internet were, by far, the greatest in number. I remember, for example, the day when Portugal Telecom had to increase the number of lines it made available for all of the free of charge messages to the UN so as not to have its services jammed. On national sites it was very easy to find direct links to the White House and other centers of power.

In the meantime, the Portuguese legislative elections of 10 October 1999 and their respective campaigns were drawing near. From the beginning, a behavior code and an interpretation of reality in respect to East Timor were established.On the one hand, it was said that electoral and party advantages could not be gained from the events in and about East Timor. On the other hand, a "national consensus" that surpassed any political differences was assumed. As for the first issue, the high point was certainly when the opposition party leader of the PSD (Social Democratic Party, the opposition right-of-center party) requested that the election date be pushed back. The president, making it very clear that the cause for East Timor would be kept "pure," refused the request. He said that it should not be corrupted by politics, suggesting perhaps the "impure" nature of politics itself.

The call for a "national consensus" was by and large publicized by the organs of political power and civic institutions, leaving the opposition parties no choice but to subscribe to it. It also intensified the media's focus on East Timor and the civic movement. However, together with many others, I felt uncomfortable when the Portuguese national anthem was sung at demonstrations, or the Indonesian people were demonized and calls were made for Portuguese military intervention. Those of us who were discomforted by this nationalism felt unable to protest.

By virtue of the urgency of the circumstances, politicians and dignitaries broke protocol by displaying emotion—from the tears of the president of the Republic to the televised looks of revulsion and irritation on the faces and in the stances of those diplomats sent to New York to pressure the UN Security Council. Perhaps the epitome was the figure of Ana Gomes, from the Bureau of Portuguese Interests in Indonesia, whom the Portuguese got used to seeing on TV, irritated, angry, and emotional. There, in the belly of the enemy, she stood defiant against him. She was the concentrated image of a morally intransigent femaleness. She showed great tenderness and intimacy with proindependence leader Xanana Gusmão when she visited him in prison and welcomed him on the day of his release, 7 September 1999.

The whole of the movement, by its very character as a mission to generate consensus, concentrated on the demand that the United Nations intervene in East Timor and on the accusation of passivity on the part of the "international community," especially the United States, but also by the other permanent members of the Security Council. The Indonesian political and military leaders were demonized: B. J. Habibie, Ali Alatas, and Wiranto. Clinton was also turned into a dishonorable figure and ridiculed through the invocation of the Monica Lewinski affair. Comparisons were made between the situation in East Timor and the claimed illegitimacy of the intervention in Kosovo.

A few questions remain to be addressed. In the first place, who initiated these events? Although much of the answer is contained in the above description, it is worth remembering that the explicit actors calling these events were always civic associations, non-governmental associations (NGOs), trade unions, and student associations. The Roman Catholic Church, associated with an important sector of the independence movement in East Timor, kept a lower profile than expected. Governmental organs were surpassed by civilian initiatives, and political parties were careful not to become protagonists, although some days before and after the elections there were speculations about who would profit from the mobilization. In addition to the crowds' spontaneous enthusiasm, grassroots organizations and activists engaged in extensive, nonpartisan forms of protest activity.

Finally, what symbolic resources were mobilized? Apart from those already mentioned, the symbolism of suffering was used much more than that of aggression: crosses, blood or red paint, candles, vigils, and mourning. The image of Xanana Gusmão became symbolically equivalent to those of Che Guevara or Nelson Mandela. This could be seen in the iconography produced in stickers, T-shirts and other kinds of political merchandising. East Timorese symbols—especially the flag—were appropriated. In terms of music, however, it was above all the song "Por Timor" (For Timor) by the Portuguese band Trovante, written on the occasion of the Santa Cruz Massacre in 1991 (see below), that was interpreted as an authentic East Timorese hymn, although it was "made in Portugal" rather than originating from East Timor itself.

One symbol perhaps dominated: the new designation for East Timor, "Timor Loro Sae," the name proposed by Xanana Gusmão after his release from prison in Jakarta. Anticipating the results of the referendum and the constitution of an independent East Timor, Xanana Gusmão said that the new nation would be called Timor Loro Sae, meaning, in the native Tetum language, "Timor of the Rising Sun" (i.e., Eastern). Not only did the expression not become current amongst the East Timorese resistance forces or the East Timorese diaspora, but there also appears to be disagreement as to its future use in East Timor. However, the media picked up the term and spread it like a virus. It became a politically correct expression and an indicator of adherence to the cause. It replaced the more prosaic and commonly used "East Timor" and avoided the term of colonial times, "Timor," as a general category that designated the whole island, not just its eastern part.

I conclude this part by admitting to a frustration: that of not being able to bring to this text the hundreds of pages of text and photos from the press, the hundreds of hours of television and radio reporting, and all of the sites on the Internet having to do with the events surrounding East Timor. But as an anthropologist doing an ethnographic report without recourse to interviews with an array of participants, I am struck by the ambiguity that characterized the discourses and the actions of the mobilization. They revealed a fascination with the Lusophone aspects of the East Timorese, including their Catholicism, and their supposed adoration for Portugal, which relieved the guilt felt by the Portuguese over their colonial past. Apart from the genuine solidarity of the movement, from the lesson of resistance and struggle exemplified in the East Timorese, apart even from the opportunity this movement gave to citizens to express their discontent with globalization, national politics, and the absence of participation in it, the question remains: why East Timor (and not Angola, for example)? What place does East Timor occupy in the Portuguese imagination? What "Timor" is this—beyond and despite East Timor—that the Portuguese have been constructing? On 25 April 1974 the Portuguese freed themselves from a dictatorship and accepted the independence of the colonies. What was happening now, twenty-five years later? My interpretation of the events is that what was at stake—more than the demand for intervention, the questioning of the "new world order," or the demonstration of a strong affective bond of solidarity for the East Timorese—was a national catharsis around issues of colonialization, decolonialization, and the reconfiguration of national identity through new processes of participatory politics.

East Timor, Indonesia, and Portugal: Colonial and Postcolonial Entanglements

A presentation of the context of the September 1999 events is more productive if it transgresses the traditional regional criteria of many fields of scholarship, including anthropology: Indonesia, East Timor, Portugal, and the "new international order" must be analyzed together. The island of Timor—comprising East and West Timor—lies in the Indonesian archipelago, an area that has experienced European expansion since the beginning of the sixteenth century. For the following three hundred years, the Portuguese and the Dutch were the main protagonists in the struggle to control commerce in the archipelago. According to Nancy Lutz (1995), the real local power was in the hands of a *mestiço* class called Topasses, or "Black Portuguese," who played an important social role.

The weakness of Portuguese colonialism and the distance between East Timor and the metropolis meant that the Portuguese never effectively colonized Timor. As a consequence of the process of concentrating resources in other colonies, the island was marginalized. Thus, in 1859 the Portuguese general headquarters was moved to East Timor when Solor and Flores were sold to the Dutch. During the nineteenth and twentieth centuries, and only very gradually, Portugal gained control of the colony, thanks largely to the introduction of coffee as an export cash crop in 1815. East Timor, however, has a history of rebellion against Portuguese rule, as testified by uprisings in 1870–92 and a rebellion in 1959. The construction of the notion of a special bond between East Timor and Portugal during the 1999 events in Lisbon was only possible on the basis of selective forgetting (of both these rebellions and the anticolonial movement)—a common procedure in the construction of collective memory.

The Portuguese presence, with an ineffective colonial administration, depended in large measure on the influence of the Catholic Church. In the section of the archipelago they controlled, the Dutch capitalized on the centrality of the island of Java and its ancient empires. They were later confronted with a national independence movement that started in the beginning of the century and continued until independence was gained in 1945. A new nation and regional power, Indonesia, emerged.

The political project of the Indonesian independence leader, Soekarno, was the unification of the archipelago. The principal cultural instrument used was linguistic: the establishment of Bahasa Indonesia as the national language in the place of Dutch. Soekarno's power depended on a balance between the influential Communist Party and the military caste—the latter being the base of the unity of the new state, as in many other new former colonized nations. Soeharto—commander of the Strategic Army Reserve—launched a coup in 1965 and established the New Order. This new, anticommunist regime was based on the introduction of army officers into civil service posts, thus militarizing the administration.

Meanwhile, the Portuguese presence continued in the eastern section of Timor, which remained a small colony of a country practicing a backward, persistent colonialism. For a long time, Portuguese colonialism was actually surrogated because the power behind Portuguese interests were the stronger states within the international economy, especially Britain.[6] After the demise of the British Empire, Portuguese colonialism continued as a political project tied to the maintenance of the dictatorship and its isolationism. Although colonies such as Angola and Mozambique became economically significant in the late colonial period, East Timor was important primarily as a symbol of the cohesion and continuity of the Empire.

After the 1955 conference of Non-Aligned Countries in Bandung, Indonesia, Portugal was obliged to change its colonial policy in order to become a member of the United Nations. This was done by changing the designation "colonies" to "overseas provinces" and by adopting the rhetoric that the Empire was a unified national and multicultural community—a fact that marked the beginning of the influence and political impact of Gilberto Freyre's theories of "Luso-Tropicalism."[7]

In 1965 Portugal was subjected to an authoritarian regime and international anticolonialist pressures, at the same time that it was also engaged in war on three fronts: Angola, Mozambique, and Guinea-Bissau. Goa, Damão, and Diu (then "Portuguese India") had already become part of India. Finally, on 25 April 1974, young military officers who were fighting in the colonial wars led a prodemocracy military coup against the Salazar-Caetano dictatorship. The coup, which was motivated by opposition to colonialism, dictatorship, and underdevelopment, and by the international isolation of Portuguese dictatorship, ended Portuguese colonialism.

According to Costa Pinto (1999), East Timor represented the most extreme case of the crossroads of Portuguese decolonialization. A small territory of a merely symbolic importance to Portugal, East Timor did not experience a full-fledged war of independence, such as those waged in the African colonies. Instead, three East Timorese political parties arose. The first, UDT (Timorese Democratic Union), defended the idea of a progressive autonomy within the framework of a Portuguese-speaking community. The ASDT / FRETILIN party (Timorese Social Democratic Association / Timorese National Liberation Front) defended independence with a transition period of three to eight years. Finally, the APODETI (People's Democratic Association of East Timor) party defended integration with Indonesia with some form of autonomy for East Timor.

In 1975 Portugal affirmed East Timor's right to self-determination. On 28 November 1975, with an Indonesian invasion imminent, FRETILIN issued the Unilateral Declaration of East Timor's Independence. The Portuguese authorities, with a weak military force, had already moved to the island of Ataúro on 27 August of the same year. The Indonesian army invaded in December 1975 (Oliveira 1996: 161–165) and by July of 1976 had completed the formal integration of East Timor into Indonesia. Portugal recognized neither the independence nor the Indonesian occupation. Until the referendum in 1999, the UN recognized Portugal as the "administrating power of a non-autonomous territory," since an internationally recognized decolonialization process had not occurred.

The Indonesian invasion was carried out under the pretext of avoiding the spread of a communist threat in the region. In the framework of international relations at the time, Indonesia was a strong ally of the United States, which, along with other governments and the Portuguese government's tacit recognition, supported the invasion. At that time, the Portuguese former colonies were anti-American threats, as was, in its revolutionary jubilation, the former metropolis itself. Without a doubt, however, the oil wells and the potential for liquid natural gas off the Timor coast also played an important role, especially for Australia, the other party that found the Indonesian invasion convenient. After the Indonesian invasion, three important developments took place: the growth of an East Timorese resistance movement (as an aftermath of the anticolonial movement, inside and outside the territory), as part of a strengthening of East Timorese nationalism; a crisis in the Indonesian regime; and the creation of an East Timorese agenda in postrevolutionary Portuguese politics and society.

The Indonesian occupation and the physical near annihilation of the resistance ended up uniting the East Timorese political forces. Throughout the period 1975–80, Indonesian military campaigns were massive, as were forced migration and hunger. This is the period that has been labeled by the Portuguese public opinion and the media as the period of genocide. Besides the guerrilla warfare in the mountains, the resistance built support outside the territory. With the help of a network of elite East Timorese in diaspora, they articulated their position convincingly with NGOs, political lobbies, the media, and diplomats, thus swaying public opinion in their favor. They also organized a third, less explicit front, joining together with collaborators with the Indonesian regime, which would eventually break with the occupiers during the crisis that would overthrow Soeharto.

In May 1998 Indonesia went into a full-scale crisis. The fall of the Berlin Wall, the new international order, and the crisis in capitalistic growth in Southeast Asia brought about a new situation. It was one in which the United States could call for the democratization of the military regimes it had supported. Australia, the preferred ally of Indonesia, had recently engaged in a burgeoning role as a regional power, and was thus gradually withdrawing its support. B. J. Habibie replaced Soeharto, initiating the nation's transition to a democratic regime, a transition that is not yet complete.

Portugal had meanwhile ended its revolution by 1975 and had begun "democratic normalization," with a return to a market economy and the preparation for incorporation into the European Union. In the context of the global restructuring of capitalism, the independence of the colonies did not decrease opportunities for Portuguese private and public investment, at the same time that financial aid for infrastructure development was injected into Portugal from the EU. Simultaneously, the old colonial rhetoric, now rephrased as universalism, nonracist humanism, miscegenation, and "cultural encounter," continued to be a structuring element of Portuguese official and commonsense narratives of identity and self-representation.

Meanwhile the East Timorese question remained the subject of quite fierce national debates. Conservative factions always underlined the "irresponsible" nature of the Portuguese decolonialization, which led to the disaster of Indonesian occupation, and the more left-wing factions could do little more than romanticize the mountain guerrilla warriors. The greatest support for the East Timorese cause came from sectors linked to the Catholic Church.

Of Language and Religion:
National Identity in the Ex-Colony and the Ex-Metropolis

For Portugal and the world, the massacre in the Santa Cruz cemetery in 1991 marked the turning point for the East Timorese question, bringing it front and center. In November of that year, Indonesian soldiers opened fire on a peaceful demonstration in Dili, killing several people, mostly students, in the Santa Cruz cemetery. The fact that British journalist Max Stahl filmed the events unleashed a process of international mobilization, which culminated in Ramos-Horta (of the CNRT, Timorese National Resistance Council) and Bishop Ximenes Belo winning the Nobel Peace Prize in 1996 as representatives of the people of East Timor. In Portugal the images of people in despair as they prayed in what was interpreted as being Portuguese[8] endowed the event with an almost religious aura and planted the seeds of an affective identification. In the Portuguese eyes, East Timor was represented as Catholic and Lusophone (Portuguese-speaking), contrary to the evidence that the majority of the population does not speak Portuguese.

A social and cultural characterization of the principal actors in the leadership of the East Timorese nationalist movement is key to understanding its postcolonial character. Beginning in the 1960s a small, educated elite with nationalist (or regionalist) aspirations started to express their ideas in the Catholic East Timorese press. This elite was in large measure a product of Catholic schools and especially the seminaries of Dare (near Dili) and São José (in Macao). Some administrators and bureaucrats, as well as some rural property owners became important leaders for both UDT and ASDT/FRETILIN. The Church constituted, on the one hand, the principal Portuguese presence of a continuous sort, and at the same time, given its transnational nature, a link between the territory and the rest of the world. Due to the fragility of Portuguese colonialism, local education was in the hands of the Church. After the Indonesian invasion, influences within the Church in the United States and Europe were able to safeguard the autonomy of the East Timorese Church and not integrate it into the Indonesian one, as the Vatican wanted. This may have allowed for the creation of an authentic national church.

In Portugal images of the East Timorese praying, and doing so supposedly in Portuguese, were motivating tropes for the affective bonding of the Portuguese to the East Timorese cause. The issue of Lusophony has arisen in the Portuguese postcolonial period and after incorporation into the European Union, as a grand theme for reconfiguring a Portuguese global identity. This process is nothing if not ambiguous in its oscillation between a neocolonialist ethos, and a multinational political project aligned against the American hegemonic project of imposing neoliberal global capitalism. The Portuguese media—especially during the September 1999 civic mobilization period—insisted *ad nauseam* on forms of linguistic identification.They equally insisted on finding, in East Timor, testimonials to a special affection toward Portugal.

This idea was conveniently reinforced by the fact that the leaders of the East Timorese resistance inside and out of the territory were part of the Lusophone elite formed during colonial times. Although speculative, the question of "racial" identification, given the *mestiço* phenotype of these leaders, cannot be ruled out, either. As the spokespeople of the movement, they easily captured Lusophone sympathies. But they were a minority and the Indonesian government actually used this image to discredit them, just as the selective perception of the Portuguese media used it for the opposite purpose. What is, however, the real dimension of the linguistic question? I wish to link this question to that of the emergence of East Timorese nationalism: both issues are marked by an originality that I classify as postcolonial.[9]

Lutz (1995) reviews the ethnolinguistic complexity of East Timor: 12 mutually incomprehensible local languages, four of them Australian and eight non-Australian, which can be divided into 35 dialects and subdialects. Tetum functions as a *lingua franca* of sorts. During the colonial period Portuguese was the official language and a prerequisite for citizenship, according to a policy of "assimilation." Following the colonial categories, in 1950 the population (in a sum total of 442,378) was made up of 568 Europeans, 2,022 *mestiço*, 3,128 Chinese, 212 other nonindigenous (from Goa, etc.), 1,541 "civilized indigenous," and 434,907 "non-civilized indigenous" persons (Weatherbee 1966: 684). To sum up, less than 1 percent of the population was "civilized," *mestiço* and Lusophone. In East Timor the social order was "typically Iberian" (Anderson 1993): beneath the Portuguese directors, there were the Chinese merchants, the *mestiços* (of local, Arab, African and Portuguese origin), and a large, diverse group of native ethnolinguistic communities.

It was precisely the above-mentioned small elite that led the resistance or served as intermediaries to the Indonesian occupiers. And it was members of this elite who emerged as representatives for an independent East Timor. According to Lutz, in the 1974–76 period, FRETILIN, drawing on Paulo Freire's model, encouraged a Tetum literacy campaign, the leaders of which were, nevertheless, primarily Portuguese speakers. On his October 1999 stopover in Lisbon, Xanana Gusmão said on national television that he composed poems in Portuguese, for that was the language in which he felt, and admitted to not having always mastered the Tetum language.

One should not forget, however, that Tetum was used before the Indonesian invasion as a form of resistance to Portuguese colonialism and that the leadership of the independence movements went beyond the *assimilado* elite.[10] As a matter of fact, Portuguese colonialism promoted a bilingual policy, with Portuguese targeted at *assimilados*, leaving the field open for Tetum as the language of the folk—a situation that provided the foundation for the Catholic Church's further popularizing Tetum as the language of liturgy. Thus a situation of diglossia could be a good description for East Timor: one in which Portuguese was for the *assimilados*, Tetum for the *gentios* or heathen (see Ferguson 1985).

After the Indonesian invasion, Portuguese was abolished and Bahasa Indonesia implemented. Lutz suggests that this was done not so much out of nationalist concerns, or even due to a focusing on criteria of citizenship, as during colonial times, but more as a measure of control, the reflection of a Foucaultian kind of governmentality. In fact, Indonesia built schools at an accelerated pace. Indonesia used the argument of national development, contrasting its politics to Portuguese neglect, as the justification for the benefits of integration—an argument that even the Portuguese acknowledged. In this process, the Church protested against "Indonesianization." Given the prohibition of Portuguese, in 1981 the Church got approval from the Vatican to hold Mass in Tetum. Lutz defends the idea—which is seconded by official Indonesian documents—that the teaching of Bahasa Indonesia was directed by security concerns. Portuguese would be a challenge to governmentality. It would represent a secret language, and thus an everyday form of resistance, "a weapon for the weak," in the sense that Scott (1985) gives it. Benedict Anderson's (1993) argument, writing about East Timor, moves in a similar direction but asks the bigger question: how did East Timorese nationalism arise?

The question is provocative. In Portugal, the general notion was that East Timorese nationalism came about on its own, flowing from the fact that the Timorese were perceived as both Lusophone and Lusophile. In reality, in the first years of Indonesian occupation, Portugal could be accused of having simply abandoned East Timor. But starting from the 1980s the East Timorese "fever" in Portugal coincided with a growing and more articulate East Timorese nationalism. Anderson—who observed the facts from the Indonesian side—said the problem was how to integrate East Timor into the national narrative. This national narrative stipulated how Indonesia was to incorporate the many ethnolinguistic and religious groups passed down from the Dutch East Indies. Unity would be secured by the historic experience and by mythology, especially around the fight against the Dutch and the myth of precolonial states, particularly as exemplified by the Javanese Majapahit of the fourteenth and fifteenth centuries.[11]

East Timor constituted a problem: it didn't have a history of struggle against the Dutch, nor did it have solid contacts with the Indonesians (given the isolation in which East Timor was kept by the Portuguese and the preference given to intraimperial links, especially with Goa, Macao, and Mozambique). The alternative, a bioethnic essentialism stressing the common "racial" origins of the peoples of the region, was not put into play, as it might not bode well for relations with the Philippines and Malaysia. According to Anderson, this could be why the Indonesians themselves were incapable of imagining the East Timorese as Indonesians. But policy in occupied East Timor was state and army-directed, not based on stereotypes prevalent in the Indonesian population. The argument of East Timorese "ingratitude"—which was to become a rhetorical standard in Indonesian official discourse—replicated the previous argument made by the Dutch in relation to the Indonesians themselves. The accusation of treason or betrayal was not leveled against the East Timorese as it was against other regional Indonesian dissidents.

Indonesian nationalism arose at the end of the nineteenth and beginning of the twentieth centuries when the Dutch began to expand the teaching of Dutch, local press, and development projects (Anderson 1993). Thus, the Indonesian nationalist leaders learned their own nativeness through the eyes of their colonizers. It was in the Dutch language that they understood what a colonial system was, as well as what its possible overthrow might be. Anderson argues that something similar could have been the case for East Timor. If nationalism, according to him, was almost nonexistent in 1974, the situation changed dramatically after the Indonesian occupation. According to Anderson, we come upon the ironic logic of colonialism: the expansion of the colonial state—in this case, Indonesia—with its new schools and development projects, engenders a profound feeling of community.

In addition, the definition of Indonesia that emerged from the anticommunist massacres of 1965–66 was also seen as part of a fight against atheism. The obligation of every Indonesian to select one of the world religions was stipulated. According to Anderson (and, I add, contrary to what the Portuguese commonly believe) in 1975 a majority of the East Timorese practiced indigenous religions, the Catholic population having more than doubled only in the last seventeen years. Beyond the fact that the Church chose to use the Tetum language, which had nationalizing effects, the Church also offered protection by the very logic of the Indonesian state itself, which sponsored and supported the main religions of Islam, Christianity, and Hinduism. In addition, Catholicism reinforced an expression of common suffering among the people.[12] For Anderson this is what substituted for the nationalism of print capitalism,[13] lacking in East Timor.

Parallel to this, another colonial irony can be pointed out: if for the Indonesian intellectuals the language of the colonizer is what permitted communication within the colony and access to modernity, in East Timor the dissemination of literacy in Bahasa Indonesia permitted the new generations to get in touch with the world beyond Indonesia. Additionally it was from this generation that the resistance had its largest recruiting base (it was always with unacknowledged discomfort that young East Timorese refugees were shown on television arriving in Lisbon unable to speak any Portuguese; in the reporting done in September 1999, newscasters always sought comments from older people who spoke some Portuguese).

At the end of October 1999, the CNRT decided that Portuguese would be the official language of the country and Tetum the "national language." The decision was contested, since a great number of youths do not speak Portuguese. In another contested strategic decision, the U.S. dollar was adopted as the new currency. In this instance, Portuguese diplomacy "lost the battle" of the escudo and the euro. CNRT's decision to adopt Portuguese as the official language was very unpopular, widening gaps between generations, men and women, and rural and urban populations. One could say that it put back in place colonial divides, given the small numbers of Portuguese speakers when compared to those of Tetum or Bahasa Indonesia. However, Bahasa Indonesia was the "enemy" language that had been historically imposed and that the leaders wanted to marginalize (see Crockford 2000).

Back to Lisbon, Back to Empire?

The civic movement in Lisbon was not a univocal one. This was noticeable from the start, from its nonpartisan character and in the confluence of "the people," be they Catholic or agnostic, from the right or the left. The creation of a "national consensus" permitted side-by-side (and not necessarily incompatible) demonstrations to take place, which were staged to attract international solidarity and yet had a subtext of colonial nostalgia. The religious identification can be seen simultaneously as an emotive force for the creation of transnational solidarity that had as its subject a Lusocentric and potentially nationalistic discourse. The international context of the new world order allowed for arguments from "the left"— anti-global capitalism—and from "the right"—nationalism—to coincide. But a set of unresolved issues were common to all, including the place of the memory of colonialism in the construction of a national identity and the traumatic place of decolonialization (liberating and progressive but recognizably poorly executed). And all actors share the dilemma that Portugal is itself simultaneously a part of the center – as a member of the European Union – and a peripheral country within this emerging power. Finding itself peripheral within the European Union, Portugal relocates itself within a global framework as the center of the Lusophone community.

What the events in East Timor, Indonesia, and Portugal reveal is a threefold postcolonial irony that can be added to the colonial ironies pointed out by Anderson: (1) nationalism in the former colony (East Timor) uses the culture of the colonizer as a mobilizing symbol for action (anti-colonial feelings notwithstanding); (2) a new Third World nation (Indonesia) becomes a regional power and invades another colony, thus encountering the limits of its own national narrative; (3) the former colonizing nation also reconfigures its identity in the midst of ambiguous nostalgia as being in solidarity with "the outpost of the Empire" that it had neglected the most.

The former colonial power becomes the principal defender of the former colony's struggle for independence. This was possible because, in between, a new colonizer (Indonesia) interceded, allowing the Portuguese to reconstruct a memory of colonial times by means of the selective forgetting of colonialism. For anthropologists worried about the weaknesses of the emergent postcolonial paradigm, this case—with its focus on affect, language, religion, and symbols and these in direct association with political events marked by injustice, violence, and nationalism—points to the complexity of studying the mutual constitution of colonizers and colonized, ex-colonizers and ex-colonized.

The area of postcolonial studies has been marked by a concentration on topics around hybridism and the dependency of postcolonial societies on the representations of the "natives" by the colonizers for their self-construction. But little has been done in some areas that seem important to me: (1) the reconfiguration of the former colonial metropolis after the independence of their colonies; (2) the comparison between the diverse colonial experiences; in this comparison the singularities of Portuguese expansion and colonialism could render more sophisticated the discussion of postmodern identities and at the same time (and it is here that the contribution of postcolonial studies is important) "modernize" the eternally parochial discussion on Portuguese exceptionalism; (3) the empirical and ethnographic study of processes of identity reconfiguration conditioned by political economy and relations of power, without subscribing to the primacy of representation and discourse.

The central question raised by the events portrayed at the beginning of this chapter is why East Timor (and not Angola, for example)? What place does it occupy in the Portuguese collective imagination? We have seen that religion and language were central in Portuguese identification with the East Timorese cause. This identification denied, however, counterevidence, the presence of the voice of the East Timorese, who are the active cultural makers of East Timorese national identity, and the confrontational aspects of colonialism. During the events of September 1999, the Portuguese *imagined* East Timor. Its small size, its distance, the existence of a big, dictatorial, and Muslim enemy (Indonesia), and the denunciation of an unjust international order in which the strong (the United States) fail to protect the weak were the narrative elements for the construction of a mythical place. Any narrative of East Timor made in Portugal is a narrative of Portugal, its colonial experience, and postcolonial reconfiguration.

The events of September 1999 in Portugal also allowed for a catharsis of all those feelings of guilt about the devastation and war left by the processes of Portuguese colonialization and decolonialization. As a psychodrama of the reconfiguration of postcolonial identity, the events had the right stuff at the right time—the stuff with which the nation could start to question the validity of making its collective project that of joining affluent European society as a "poor cousin" and to search for alternatives within the old identity discourses (inseparable from an expansionist and colonialist narrative). The Portuguese state has been implementing a politics of representation and identity that focuses on language (Lusophony) as the unifying factor for both the Portuguese diaspora and the former colonies. Empire seems, thus, to have been replaced by language. Whether the Portuguese subscribed to this politics or not remains to be seen in further developments, but the September 1999 events constitute an omen.

Notes

1. A similar version of this essay was published in *Identities*, Vol. 8 (9): 583–605.

2. The dictatorship was overthrown in 1974: the "revolution" encompasses the subsequent period of struggle between moderates and radicals, from April 1974 to November 1975, approximately.
3. In his discussion of liminality, Turner says: "I prefer the Latin term *communitas* to 'community,' to distinguish this modality of social relationship from an 'area of common living.' The distinction between structure and *communitas* is not simply the familiar one between 'secular' and 'sacred,' or that, for example, between politics and religion" (1969: 96). This "communitas," he says, "...emerges recognizably in the liminal period, ... society as an unstructured or rudimentarily structured and relatively undifferentiated comitatus, community, or even communion of equal individuals ..." (1969: 96).
4. Fado is a traditional popular urban singing style that was highly supported and promoted by Salazar's dictatorial regime (1926–74). It has been interpreted by the left-wing intelligentsia as a cultural product that reproduces Portuguese cultural notions of nostalgia, acceptance of fate, and the valuing of suffering. Marginalized after the 1974–75 revolution, Fado made its way back into the center stage of representations of the national character and cultural authenticity in the 1990s.
5. It was also proposed that United States Avenue be renamed Timor Loro Sae Avenue.
6. This was particularly the case with Mozambique, which was "sublet" to Britain and, later, to South Africa, through mechanisms of labor export.
7. The ideas of Gilberto Freyre, the author of the classic analysis of Brazilian slavery, *The Masters and the Slaves* (1933), were appropriated by the official propaganda of the dictatorial and colonial Portuguese regime throughout the 1950s and 1960s. See chapter 3.
8. But could easily have been Tetum, the language of Catholic liturgy in East Timor.
9. In the sense that it is posterior to colonialism and to the failure of national liberation movements (such as the Indonesian), based on an anticolonial logic, to end foreign domination and win meaningful sovereignty.
10. *Assimilados* (literally "assimilated") were colonial natives who spoke Portuguese, practiced Catholicism, and could work in the administration. They were seen by the colonial regime as the ultimate product of a process of "civilization."
11. See Geertz (1980) on Indonesian political mythology.
12. A similar process occurred in nineteenth-century Ireland. This may help explain the force of the pro-Timorese movement in Ireland, the largest next to Portugal's. The identification between national identity and Catholicism is obvious, as well as the transnational connections the latter can trigger.
13. See Anderson (1983).

6
PITFALLS AND PERSPECTIVES IN ANTHROPOLOGY, POSTCOLONIALISM, AND THE PORTUGUESE-SPEAKING WORLD

This chapter is an attempt to situate the vantage point of a Portuguese anthropologist who is looking at his country's colonial past and at where his discipline stands in times of "postcolonial" concerns. In what regards empirical material, it stands halfway between fieldwork done in Brazil (see Vale de Almeida 2000, and chapter 2 in this book) and forthcoming work on constructions of creoleness and hybridity in colonial and postcolonial times.

The first part, "The Invention of the Post-Colony," introduces postcolonial studies, and proceeds into a critique of the postcolonial fashion. The second part tackles the issue of "Anthropology and Postcolonialism." The third part focuses on "The Portuguese Colonial Experience": it explores the heuristic value of the notion of "the Black Atlantic" and experiments with that of "the Brown Atlantic." Finally, the concluding remarks focus on "Postcolonialism in Portuguese: Race, Culture, and Nation."

The Invention of the Post-Colony

The field of postcolonial studies has challenged anthropologists concerned with the politics of identity in the context of globalization. This challenge echoes that previously set forth by cultural studies. They are both inter- (or should one say trans-?) disciplinary efforts triggered by the awareness of identity ambiguity and/or multiculturalism felt by the field's scholars themselves. Anthropologists tend to feel that their discipline is more apt to convey meaning and explanation of identity transformation processes, and that situations of ambiguity and/or multiculturalism are empirical facts that need to be identified as such in our informants' lives, not taken-for-granted situations or products of political wishful thinking. Postcolonial studies, in particular, is challenging to anthropologists because we are "specialists" in former colonized populations and/or in minority or migrant communities—the very stuff of postcolonial studies' concern.

It is a well-established fact that postcolonial studies emerged from within literary criticism and cultural studies. In the Anglo-Saxon context they were triggered by the critique of the notion of commonwealth literature.[1] Under the influence of poststructuralism and critical theory, the British cultural studies were no longer to pay attention mainly to English working-class identity, but would eventually focus also on the growing immigration from the former colonies and the constitution of a multicultural society. At the same time, the search for a noncolonial and alternative historiography in India (with the Subaltern Studies Group), and the influx of diaspora scholars influenced by negritude and pan-Africanism, set the conditions for the emergence of what was to be known as postcolonial studies. The attention to the organization of historiography as a narrative, as well as the influence of Saïd's (1978) analysis of Orientalism, was the watermark of the field. But so were its objects: narratives, discourses, and literature.

Prakash (1997) asserts that one of the effects of postcolonial criticism has been the introduction of a radical critique of patterns of knowledge and social identities, which were authored and authorized by colonialism and Western dominance. This does not mean that colonialism and its legacies have remained unquestioned until today (one needs only to think of nationalism and Marxism), but rather that both operated with master narratives, which placed Europe at the center. Postcolonial criticism would, therefore, try to undo Eurocentrism, while keeping the awareness that postcoloniality does not develop in panoptical distance from history: postcoloniality exists as an "after"—after having been "worked over" by colonialism. The space occupied by this enunciation of discourses of domination is neither inside nor outside the history of European domination, but rather in a tangential relationship to it; this would be Bhabha's (1994) "in between" or hybrid position, one of practice and negotiation, or what Spivak (1990) called catachresis: to revert, dislocate, and attack the apparatus of value coding. As Ashcroft (1998) puts it, postcolonialism deals with the effects of colonization in societies and cultures, not in a strict chronological, postindependence sense.

This shallow definition hides the turmoil generated by this new approach. Social scientists, once confronted with this "takeover" of their objects of concern (and here I think mainly of anthropologists), criticized the excessive focus on representations and discourse. Some would catalogue the new field as a fad or a new academic niche—a result of academic politics.

Possibly the most often quoted attack on postcolonial studies is that by Dirlik (1994). The author feels that postcolonialism claims as its own the field that was previously known as the "Third World," with the purpose of collapsing distinctions of the center-periphery kind, and other allegedly colonialist "binarisms." The postcolonial tag supposedly was used in the 1980s to describe Third World scholars, thus confusing an unspecified group with a global condition. Dirlik argues that:

1. there is a parallel between the rise of the "postcolonial" idea and the consciousness emerging from global capitalism in the 1980s:
2. the issues in postcolonial criticism have to do with conceptual needs in the transformations in global relations due to changes in the capitalist world economy. This would have led to the concept's complicity in the consecration of hegemony.

Dirlik also identifies the various uses of the expression:

1. as a description of the conditions of former colonial societies, whether Third World or settler colonies such as Canada and Australia;
2. as a description of a global condition after colonialism;
3. as a description of a discourse about the above-mentioned conditions. The question "How can the Third World write its own history?" asked by the Subaltern Studies Group supposedly started the process.

The main characteristics of the postcolonial trend would therefore be, according to Dirlik:

1. the refusal of all master narratives;
2. the critique of the Eurocentrism implicit in them;
3. the main master narrative is modernization, whether in its bourgeois or Marxist version;
4. the refusal of Orientalism, as well as of nationalism as a reduction to an essence without history;
5. the refusal of all foundational history;
6. the refusal of any fixation of the Third World subject and of the former as a category;
7. the assertion of Third World identities as relational rather than essential, shifting attention from "national origin" to "subject position."

This implies that the First/Third world positions are very fluid and that local interactions are more important than the global structures that format those relations. These conclusions would proceed from the hybrid or in-between character of the postcolonial subject, thus establishing a global condition as a projection of subjectivity in the world. Dirlik concludes his criticism saying that this is a discursive constitution of the world. He believes the term excludes all those who, unaware of their hybridism, keep on massacring each other in ethnic, religious, and national conflicts; it excludes those radicals who say that their societies are still colonized; and it especially excludes indigenous activists who do not accept the repudiation of essentialized identities. He quotes O'Hanlon and Washbrook (1992) to stress his point:

> The solutions it offers—methodological individualism, the depoliticizing insulation of social from material domains, a vision of social relations that is in practice extremely voluntaristic, the refusal of any kind of programmatic politics—do not seem to us radical, subversive or emancipatory. They are ... conservative and implicitly authoritarian... (Dirlik 1997: 514)

This highly politicized criticism echoes that by Jameson (1984) of postmodernism. He had found a relation between postmodernism and a new phase in the development of capitalism, one in which (due to a series of characteristics better described recently by Castells [1997]), for the first time, the capitalist mode of production appears as a global abstraction, divorced from its European conditions of emergence. The narrative of capitalism would no longer be a European narrative. The situation created by global capitalism would help explain certain phenomena that occurred in the 1980s, namely the global movements of people, the replication within societies of inequalities that were previously related to colonial differences, the global-local interpenetration, and the disorganization of a world conceived in three or in nation-states.

This criticism could equally apply to general theoretical trends associated with postmodern and poststructuralist thought in general. However, behind (and beyond) theory, there is the fact that most of the world lives today in a condition of in-betweenness, of which social agents are by and large aware. In sum, we are witnessing an historical change in the relationship between individuals, groups, the state, and the economy, a change that affects the symbolic resources for action by the people that we, as anthropologists, study.

Anthropology and Postcolonialism

The term "postcolonial" applies not so much to the period after independence but rather to its more recent phase (see Chatterjee 1986, 1993; Ahmad 1995; Prakash 1990; Appiah 1992; Dirlik 1997; Scott 1996). As Scott demonstrated, the postcolonial problem is an outcome of the fall of socialism and the triumph of neoliberal market economy at the planetary scale. The optimism of the anticolonial movement foundered with the shipwreck of communism, and with the feeling that the nationalist elites have betrayed the nationalistic and anticolonial cause in the former colonies.

The term has undoubtedly been overused and abused, both at the chronological and the geographical levels. Personally, I find it useful to establish some boundaries:

1. the term "postcolonial" should be applied to the period
   a. after colonialism; and
   b. after the failure of nationalist anticolonial projects implemented after independence;
2. the term should be applied to those complexes of transnational relations between former colonies and former colonizing centers;
3. all the rest—globalization, settler societies, neocolonialism, internal colonialism, and so on—are issues that should be treated in their own terms.

The usefulness of the term "postcolonial" is related to the opportunity to set forth an integrated analysis of the historical continuity and mutual constitution of social representations of colonizers and colonized, provided that:

1. there is a permanent consideration of the colonialism/postcolonialism continuum;
2. discursive analysis does not do away with considerations of political economy, which sustain the analysis of the material aspect of social processes;
3. the practice of social actors in specific contexts is analyzed, in order to achieve a better grasp of the complexities of identity negotiation;
4. there be empirical research, namely of an ethnographic nature; and
5. one uses the comparative method, namely regarding the comparison of different colonial and postcolonial experiences.[2]

This, I believe, is the only way in which the postcolonial studies approach can be reinserted into the much older anthropological tradition—one that pays attention to the Other's version of events and life.

Robotham (1997) tries to insert the postcolonial moment in an appraisal of the role and development of anthropology. As a formal discipline it was born out of the development of world markets, during the process of European expansionism and colonialism, coinciding with the strengthening of Western rationalism. The phase of imperialism in the nineteenth century was to create a new universalistic discipline, in a process in which "modernization" was confused with "Westernization." Today one may peacefully admit that anthropology carried the burden of earlier colonialist presuppositions (Asad 1973), created images of the Other as a subaltern, and gave ontological and epistemological primacy to the West (Saïd 1983)—although I would say that anthropology carried also the social potential of being a counterhegemonic discourse that presented the diverse rationalities of Others. In the aftermath of the critique of anthropology during decolonialization, a self-critical movement started. It was influenced by deconstructive and postmodern perspectives, and took place in the context of the fall of real socialism, the triumph of neoliberal globalization, the electronic revolution, and the globalization of finance and communications (see Castells 1997; Appadurai 1990).

However, Robotham says that in anthropology we have entered a period that offers countless possibilities—instead of the pessimistic stance that says that anthropology's subject has vanished, a position I subscribe to. Postmodernism declared the death of modernity's project. However, we are witnessing the denial of that idea: it is not so much a matter of modernity versus postmodernity, but rather the emergence of several new or alternative modernities (see Ong 1996), a situation that allows—maybe for the first time—for the practice of a multipolar anthropology, on behalf of humanisms and modernities that do not necessarily have to be Western. I also believe that the fact that anthropology itself was part and parcel of western expansion constitutes an added value for reflexive and critical work by anthropologists in conditions of increased and accelerated "globalization."

In a similar compromising vein, Hall (1996) starts by accepting the critique of postcolonial studies made by Shohat (1992) (and shared by McClintock [1992, 1997]). The field was criticized for its political and theoretical ambiguity, the confusion established in the distinction between colonizers and colonized, thus dissolving the politics of resistance as a consequence of not pointing out who exercises domination. Dirlik would actually add that the capitalist structuring of the world is underestimated and that a notion of discursive identity is proposed—in sum, a sort of culturalism.

Hall—and I tend to agree with him—hesitates in subscribing to either the postcolonial interpretations originating in the centers of literary criticism or the counterattacks that refuse the window of opportunities that the new field opened up. For Hall, societies are not all postcolonial in the same manner. The concept of postcolonialism will be useful only inasmuch as it may help us describe and characterize the change in global relations, which marks the unequal transition from the age of empires to the postindependence period. On the one hand, the change is universal, inasmuch as colonized and colonizing societies were both affected by the process. On the other hand, the term "postcolonial" cannot merely describe this or that, or a "before" and an "after." It should reread colonization as part of a process that is essentially transnational and translocal, thus producing a decentered, diasporic, or global writing of previous imperial grand narratives centered on nations. In this sense, postcolonialism is not a periodization based on stages.

In the same vein, Werbner and Ranger (1996) identify the African post-colony as a plurality of spheres and arenas in which the postcolonial subject mobilizes several identities that have to be constantly revised in order to acquire maximum instrumentality. Thus, the postcolonial mode of domination is as much a regime of constraints as a practice of conviviality and a style of connivance, they say, leading us into considering the multiple ways in which people "play" with power rather than confront it—in a way very similar to the rituals of rebellion analyzed by Gluckman in the 1960s. The problem, then, is to avoid a notion of Western hegemony so strong that it would lead us to the point of seeing it as the manufacturer of the very local sociability in the ex-colonies—

a real risk, whereas the anthropologist's duty is to know the everyday cultural politics of those places.

One has, therefore, to acknowledge in colonialism a source of hybridity and the "place" where the notion of ethnicity was invented. That is why it is necessary to:

1. place history first;
2. do an ethnography of ethnography;
3. do a postcolonial historical anthropology about colonial society; and
4. do an anthropology of the reconfigurations of colonial experiences in the former imperial centers.

This is particularly important in the Portuguese context, where analysis is needed for such subjects as the commemoration of Brazil's five hundred years, the invention of Lusophony, Expo 98, or the emergence of a social field marked by the pair of multiculturalism/racism.

The Portuguese Colonial Experience

The Portuguese colonial experience was for a long period tied up with the slave trade and the use of slave labor, whether in the making of Brazil or in the colonial reorientation toward Africa after that country's independence. Diasporic "Africans," mainly in the Americas (and, today, in Europe) constitute the ideal population for the analysis of contemporary processes of diaspora, transnationality, and the reemergence of ethnogenealogical discourses. After fieldwork in Brazil on the emergence of the Black movement—as both cultural and political movement—in a town of Bahia (see Vale de Almeida 2000 and chapter 2 of this book), I am now interested in analyzing the historical construction of the notion of creoleness (mainly in Cape Verde) during colonial times, and how it reproduced and/or transformed itself after the independences. Both in Brazil and Cape Verde one is confronted with discourses that proclaim the inexistence of a bipolar racial formation. This characteristic is linked to the supposedly original character of Portuguese colonization; in addition, this construct is reproduced as a structuring component of Portuguese national identity and self-representations. Reframing the issue, shifting one's attention from the "nation" to more fluid and multipolar intracolonial contexts, is probably the first step for a reanalysis of colonialism/postcolonialism from an anthropological point of view.

Paul Gilroy (1993) has been a major source of inspiration for my reflections on the postcolonial situation of the Afro-Diaspora. The Black Atlantic designates an intercultural and transnational formation characterized by the fact that racial slavery was an integral part of Western civilization and modernity. Concerned with the absence of attention to "race" and ethnicity in contemporary works on modernity—and finding little use for the polarization of essentialist and anti-essentialist theories of Black identity—Gilroy appropriates the notion of "double consciousness" once outlined by W. E. B. DuBois. It refers to the underlying difficulty in reconciling two identifications: to be simultaneously European and Black. Gilroy distrusts the two predominant attitudes in dealing with that double consciousness: on the one hand, "cultural nationalism" and other integral conceptions of culture, and on the other, the alternative of creolization, *métissage*, *mestizaje*, or hybridity. The latter are seen as unsatisfactory terms, used to refer to processes of cultural mutation and discontinuity. Focusing on the theme of music, Gilroy says that the stereophonic, bilingual, or bifocal cultural forms that originated among Blacks—but that are no longer their exclusive property—have been dispersed in "structures of feeling, producing, communicating, and remembering that [he has] heuristically called the Black Atlantic world" (1993: 3).

Being at the same time inside and outside the West—"double consciousness"—would have led to refusals of complicity and interdependence between White and Black thinkers and to the fact that many Black political struggles have been constructed as automatically expressive of the ethnic or national differences with which they are associated. For Gilroy, the essentialist and pluralist points of view are actually two varieties of essentialism: one is ontological, the other strategic. The former normally presents itself as a sort of raw pan-Africanism; the latter, by means of seeing race as a social construct, cannot explain the persistence and continuity of racialized forms of power.

In order to overcome this impasse, Gilroy proposed that the expressive counterculture—for instance, the field of music that he analyzed—be no longer seen as a mere succession of literary tropes and genres, but rather as a philosophical discourse that refuses the modern and Western separation between ethics and aesthetics, culture and politics. Thus, the move from slavery to citizenship would have taken Afro-descendants to inquire about the best forms of social existence, but the memory of slavery—preserved as an intellectual resource in their expressive political culture—led them to look for answers to that query. Those answers are different from those supplied by the liberal social contract.

This means that the concept of tradition cannot be seen as the opposite of modernity. That is why Gilroy despises Afrocentric ideas, since they are necessarily opposed to the double consciousness that so fascinated Black modernists invoked by him—especially in the U.S., the Caribbean, and the United Kingdom. In a similar vein to Clifford (1997), he proposes that one deal equally with the meaning of "roots" and "routes," so as to undermine the purifying inclination toward either Afrocentrism or Eurocentrism. Gilroy feels that the Afrocentric notion of time is too linear, placing tradition outside history, focusing on projects of "return to Africa" or ideas of racial integrity. Contrarily, the anticolonial Black intellectuals that inspired him—such as DuBois, Douglass, or Wright—periodized their conceptions of modernity in a different way: they always started with the catastrophic rupture of the Middle Passage, the processes of forced acculturation, the countercultural desires for freedom, citizenship, and autonomy. This temporality and this history constituted communities of feeling and interpretation.

In his argument about the relationship between tradition, modernity, temporality, and social memory, Gilroy says that the telling and retelling of stories organized the awareness of the "racial" group and established the balance between inside and outside activity—the diverse cognitive, habitual, and performative practices that are needed in order to invent, maintain, and renew identity. These constituted the Black Atlantic as a "nontraditional tradition," a truly modern cultural set: ex-centric, unstable, and asymmetrical, inapprehensible by a Manichean binary code. Once again, music can be used as an example: the circulation and mutation of music throughout the Black Atlantic shattered the dualist structure that placed Africa, authenticity, purity, and origin in a crude oppositional relationship to the Americas, hybridity, creolization and rootlessness. The acknowledgement of the existence of a two-way traffic (at least) leads one to change from the chronotope of "road" to that of "crossroads." Gilroy says that the "concentrated intensity" of the experience of slavery has marked Blacks as the first truly modern people, one who had to deal in the nineteenth century with the dilemmas and difficulties that would become common in Europe only a century later.

In another work, Gilroy (1996) tries to fit the Black Atlantic into notions of globalization. If the Black Atlantic is the deterritorialized, multiplex, and antinational basis for the affinity or "identity of passions" between diverse Black populations, the complex of similarity and difference that led to the consciousness of diasporic interculture has become more extensive in the age of globalization than it was in the times of imperialism. The battle goes on between those who try to put an end to the fragmentation of Africans in the diaspora, favoring the simplicity of supposed racial essences. But the diaspora should not be seen as the way out from a point of origin, but rather like something more chaotic. The obsession with the origins, which is so present in many Black thinkers, would be a kind of modernist "defect," since what Castells calls a space of flows was already prefigured in the "trialectics" of triangular commerce between Europe, Africa, and the Americas.

Gilroy's approach seems to be most useful for understanding the complex relations between colonizers and colonized, between diverse colonized people, as well as the postcolonial reproduction of those connections. That became obvious when I dealt with the production of performative culture by the Black movement in Brazil. Now, concerning the Portuguese-speaking case, to what extent and how were certain intracolonial representations reproduced across the Empire and continued into the postcolonial period?

I propose "The Brown Atlantic" as an ironic designation for the world created during the Portuguese Empire or, more accurately, for the larger hegemonic narrative of the Portuguese miscegenation project, its supposed actualization in the construction of Brazil, and its blatant failure (in spite of *a contrario* discourses) in Africa. It is also, however, a statement about specificity. Although cultural exceptionalism is refused, one must avoid "throwing away the baby with the bathwater," as the saying goes.

The postulates of postcolonial theory are not, then, fully useful for an understanding of the Afro-Diaspora, that "product" par excellence of colonialism. They seem to be more adequate to describe the situation of migratory diasporas and former colonized populations who have remained in their birthplaces. In the Luso-Brazilian and Brazilian cases (as well as in Gilroy's Black Atlantic), the colonial experience was the experience of slavery—for the whole of society but especially for Blacks. The granting of citizenship to Black Brazilians after abolition placed them in a "nonethnic" situation, different from that of indigenous populations. Their insertion in the predominantly urban class society generated close ties between "race" and class, but did not subsume the former into the latter. Whether they were classified as forms of adaptation, acculturation, syncretism, resistance, or even separatism, the fact is that large sectors of the Brazilian Black population reproduced an expressive culture and a set of common values and sentiments—including those that spread into the general society—that helped constitute an identity that can be mobilized in the arenas of struggle for power and differentiation, by means of using a set of diverse referents for identity construction: a mythical original Africa, pan-Africanism, miscegenated Brazil, racist Brazil, or Afro-Brazilianness. The present moment—marked by the creation of a democratic society in Brazil and by globalization—is witnessing the emergence of a Black Brazilian ethnicity. It involves the definition of a specific cultural heritage, presupposing forms of cultural objectification that precede cultural commodification; the plotting of a foundational narrative, including place of origin, community of experience and the historical construction of specific values; the creation of transnational ties on the basis of some global Africanness or *négritude;* and the alliance between the publicizing of products of expressive culture and the claims for political and civil rights in the democratic nation state.

In such a context it becomes risky to refer to Afro-Brazilians as part of "'Portuguese' postcolonialism." Brazil's independence in the nineteenth century, the neo-European nature of the nation-state, the time hiatus between the Atlantic triangulation among Portugal–colonial Brazil–Africa, and the Third Portuguese Empire in Africa are all aspects that suggest caution. Portuguese postcolonialism is much more that of Portugal's relations with its former colonies in Africa and with African immigrants in Portugal. In that picture, Brazil plays a phantasmagoric role in the Portuguese imagination and in official rhetoric, which has no similar equivalent in Brazilian visions of Portugal. Most equivocations of Lusophony and in the celebrations of Brazil's five hundredth anniversary originate there.[3]

On the other hand, Gilroy's analysis and propositions are excessively focused on an "Anglophone" Black Atlantic, based on the experience of the British Empire. A comparison between the colonial and postcolonial situations of Africans and their descendants who experienced different European colonial centers (which, anyway, were not equivalent: consider the subaltern character of Portuguese colonialism, for instance) is needed in order to find out to what extent we are talking about a Black Atlantic or, using a chromatic metaphor for a different shade, a Brown Atlantic in the case of Brazil. The analysis of specificity does not necessarily mean the acceptance of exceptionality—that is, of some sort of ideological Luso-Tropicalism.[4]

The main problem with the area of postcolonial studies seems to be, then, the primacy of discourse and representation. For an anthropologist, those always need to be confronted with the practice of social agents. This does not mean that some aspects of poststructuralist thought—for instance, the fragmentation of identity—should not be incorporated into anthropological thought. Furthermore, the contemporary situation of globalization makes that trend an empirical reality. However, in the face of fragmentation, several identities are reconfigured, identities that simultaneously reconstruct individuals and incorporate them into groups that are capable of mobilization for action—cultural-political action, as in the case of ethnic resurgence. The acknowledgment of the constructed nature of certain identity concepts does not mean that they exist only for our informants. That is what happens with "race," for instance, since the factual experience of exclusion is based on that form of categorization. It should not be surprising, then, that more or less mitigated forms of reactive (or strategic) essentialism emerge. Social movements are not necessarily "progressive," much less so those of a "racial" or ethnic nature.

In the Brazilian case, "double consciousness" acquires the contours of a struggle for modern civil rights and democracy and, at the same time, the struggle for the recovering and maintenance of traditions and specificities, whether invented or not. The background is inequality, as well as a disbelief in the egalitarian potential of modernity, and a belief in the liberating potential of cultural expressions, in an unstable alliance with political or social movements. Afro-Brazilians—who are neither immigrants, nor members of a diaspora with a shallow genealogical depth, nor a demographic minority or an ethnic group disputing territory with another—are confronted with the choice between an invented ethnic nationalism ("Africa in Brazil") and the struggle for racial democracy as an unaccomplished dream that was denounced as a myth. Once the obsession with the exceptional nature of Brazilian society (and of Portuguese colonialism) is overcome, as well as the dualist comparison between the racial formations of Brazil and the United States, the Afro-Brazilian case may constitute a crucial contribution for rethinking such universal questions as ethnicity and ethnopolitics, the resilience of "race," the processes of identity formation in a globalized world, or that "in-between" postcoloniality that Afro-Brazilians feel when they realize that they are simultaneously citizens and marginals, Brazilians and hyphenated Brazilians.

Brazil gained its independence in 1822. As in other South American countries, independence was achieved by and for the benefit of local elites of European origin. The demographic dimension of the Black population and the issue of slavery turned the racial and cultural crossroads into the focal point of the analyses and constructions of the nation state and national identity. Racist theories, which proclaimed the country's degeneracy due to African influences, were to be replaced by wishful-thinking appraisals of miscegenation. However, these processes never ceased to be seen as simultaneous with a desirable whitening; they did not avoid the cornering of African aspects to the field of expressive culture; and they did not challenge the maintenance of social inequalities by means of the mechanics of color prejudice (albeit not by legal segregation). Proclaimed as a racial democracy, merchandised internationally as a paradise of hybridity, the Brazilian racial formation subsists thanks to economic marginalization and a hegemonic effect, which consists in the reproduction of racial inequality at the same time that its existence is denied and its denouncers are tagged as racists themselves (Hanchard 1994).

Gilberto Freyre (see chapter 3), in the 1930s, was the ideologue of miscegenated Brazil. One can say that he set forth a premature postcolonial discourse, considering his fascination with cultural pooling and hybridization. He also made the same mistakes when seeing the hybrid as an aggregate of different "cultures," and not seeing cultural encounters as power ridden. It was the supposed exceptionality of Portuguese colonialism that produced a hybrid country. His ideas have been systematically denounced as ideological and in contradiction with the deep social inequalities that have prevailed ever since slavery. But the interesting aspect of Freyre's ideas is the fact that his interpretation of Brazil was used by the Portuguese colonial regime between 1950 and 1970, in order to justify Portugal's presence in Africa in times of decolonialization. Praised as an exceptionally humanistic, universalistic and hybridizing colonialism (on the basis of culturalist interpretations of Portugal itself), the regime used Brazil as the example to be followed in Africa.

Portuguese colonialism was undoubtedly specific:

1. There was a time gap between the colonial experience in Brazil and that in Africa. Brazil could, therefore, be used as a symbolic resource for the construction of an African empire.
2. Portuguese colonialism in Africa was subaltern, administered from a "weak" periphery, a semiperipheral country.
3. It was, for the most part, administered by dictatorial regimes.
4. It was a late colonialism that lasted beyond the independence of other European powers' colonies.
5. These factors account for the cultural negotiations between individuals and groups of European and African origin that, in the colonies, devised hybrid forms of social relations and identity in spite of bureaucratic state attempts at social boundary regulation. But one should not equate these specificities with some sort of moral and cultural exceptionalism, as Luso-Tropicalism seemed to indicate (see note 3).

Cape Verde's case highlights these trends. Both the local Creole elite and the Portuguese administration promoted the discourse of Cape Verde as a hybridized culture, and metaphorically applied this interpretation to political practice, using Cape Verdeans as business and administrative intermediaries in the other African colonies. And this occurred in spite of parallel exportation of Cape Verdean labor to semislavery in São Tomé, for instance: ideology triumphed over contradiction, and the idea of being halfway between Africa and Europe continues to have value in the archipelago. The same notion of crossroads, of multiple influences, and of transnational, deterritorialized identity making can be applied to both a colonial project and a liberating postcolonial one. Both are based on the simplistic interpretation that "racial" miscegenation carries with it intermediation, worldliness, and cosmopolitanism, provided that the underlying structures of power and inequality (namely class, but also internal racial classifications, as in both Brazil and Cape Verde) are not made explicit.

Postcolonialism in Portuguese: "Race," Culture, and Nation

Once the colonies became independent; once Portugal became a democracy within the EU; and once the socialist camp on which the former colonies depended collapsed, the postcolonial reconfiguration was on its tracks on both sides of the colonial divide. This is particularly obvious today, for several reasons:

1. the collapse of emancipatory and nationalist projects in the former colonies and the emergence of ethnic divisions;
2. the growth of African immigration to Portugal, leading to the emergence of "ethnic minorities" and manifestations of racism and antiracism;
3. in Portugal, the challenge to national identity set forth by the membership of the EU.

For the first time, Portugal does not look upon itself through its extra-European, "away-from-Spain," narrative of expansion. Or does it? For the first time the former colonies do not look upon them through the narrative of liberation from colonialism. Or do they?

Historians have made excellent efforts at a comprehensive and comparative understanding of the historical structures of Portuguese colonialism. There are also good examples of analysis of postcolonial literature, namely in Portuguese-speaking Africa, and some examples of analysis of the workings of political economy in the former colonies, mainly related to development. However, the weak anthropological effort of the Portuguese colonial enterprise seems to have been inherited by contemporary Portuguese anthropology: the anthropological analysis of the processes of colonial power-knowledge, the ethnographic approach to the former colonial fields, and the consideration of the historical continuum of the mutual constitution of the identities of colonizers and colonized are but beginning.

An anthropological analysis of Portuguese postcolonialism will have to accept the specificity of its colonial experience, but must refuse any notions of culturalist exceptionalism, freeing itself from Luso-Tropicalism, a commonsense interpretation that is rooted in nineteenth-century imperialist motivations and which was to be systematized by Freyre in the 1930s. It will have to analyze the processes of national identity formation in the former colonies, and see how the internal cleavages in each of those countries are rooted in the colonial experience. It will have to observe and analyze how transnational identity movements are made actual in ex-colonial contexts, as is the case with the Black movement in Brazil or, for instance, with the internationalization of Cape Verdean culture. It will also have to analyze what happens in Portugal in close interdependence with other issues: immigration, racism and antiracism, commemorative politics, invention of a Portuguese diaspora and of Lusophony, among others.

Portuguese colonialism, especially its Third Empire in nineteenth- and twentieth-century Africa, was built upon concepts of racial classification and separation as well as those of hybridity and miscegenation. These concepts were anchored in a previous colonial experience, that of Brazil, where the nation-state emerged as a self-proclaimed humanistic hybrid. And they have been a constitutional part of the Portuguese national narrative ever since the nineteenth century and under a variety of political regimes, as well as a conflicting part of the self-representations and national projects of the former colonies' elites. Nowadays, the culturalist trope of language and the vague notion of a common past seem to creep up as attempts to reconstitute a postcolonial entity, one that may create transnational links in order to balance the erosion effect of globalization. These attempts are, of course, in contradiction with a cold analysis of the power processes of colonialism and the structural realities of neocolonialism. It is this fuzzy and contradictory process—this muddy, earth-colored, "Brown" Atlantic— that needs to be dealt with in research.

Notes

1. Which makes one wonder whether a similar move would not be desirable in relation to the ambiguous domain of "Lusophony."
2. This perspective was the outcome of a seminar on "Colonial Tensions and Postcolonial Reconfigurations," organized by C. Bastos, B. Feldman-Bianco, and myself in Portugal (see Bastos, Vale de Almeida, and Feldman-Bianco, eds., 2002).
3. "Brown" would be the equivalent of "pardo" (an old Portuguese word for "gray") in former Anglophone colonial contexts. The word is used to define (and self-define) Brazilians who do not want to be labelled as "Black." In the chromatic idiom of racism, the Portuguese are often referred to as "dark" in comparison to their northern European counterparts.
4. I refer to the fact that the project of Lusophony—the creation of a political and cultural community of Portuguese-speaking countries—has no real acceptance in Brazil. It remains a Portuguese governmental initiative, supported by the governments of African Portuguese-speaking countries. The commemoration of the five hundred years of Brazil were the stage of conflicts between the Brazilian authorities (and their official Portuguese guests) and the Black and Indian activists.

Epilogue
A Sailor's Tale

The *Marinheiro* (the Sailor) is a central character in the Afro-Brazilian religion of *Candomblé* in Ilhéus, where I did fieldwork on the Black movement (see chapter 2). This Sailor dialogues with another "Sailor": that which Gilroy mentions in *The Black Atlantic*. Gilroy uses the symbol of ships and sailors in order to propose new chronotopes that are less tied to borders and territories. He focuses on the image of ships moving across the space between Europe, America, Africa, and the Caribbean:

> The image of the ship—a living, micro-cultural, micro-political system in motion … focus[es] attention on the middle passage, on the various projects of return to Africa, on the circulation of ideas and activists as well as the movement of key cultural and political artifacts: tracts, books, gramophone records. (1993: 4)

I would add to this geography the virtual inner sea that was formed between Bahia (Brazil) and the coast of West Africa for slave trading, the selling of Bahian tobacco in West African ports and, later, the several "returns to Africa" by many Afro-Brazilians.

The Black Atlantic formation is seen by Gilroy as rhizomorphic, as opposed to localized nationalistic perspectives. Gilroy offers numerous examples of the ship and sailor metaphors, but most importantly he says that the ship gives an indication of when modernity might have started. One of Gilroy's favorite characters is Davidson, who was a member of the Marylebone Reading Society, a radical group formed in 1819 after the Peterloo massacre. Davidson was the flag bearer of the group at a public meeting; the flag, which was black, pictured a skull and crossbones, and underneath it the motto "Let us die as men, not sold as slaves" could be read. At the end of the eighteenth century a quarter of the British Navy was composed of Africans for whom the experience of slavery must have constituted a strong motivation for embracing ideals of freedom (Gilroy 1993).

Another character, Frederick Douglass, had first heard talk of freedom from Irish sailors in the northern United States when he was working in the port of Baltimore. He was to escape captivity disguised as a sailor. But other "characters" are invoked: according to Gilroy, the involvement of Marcus Garvey, George Padmore, Claude McKay, and Langston Hughes with ships and sailors apparently gives substance to Linebaugh's (author of books on pirates) suggestion that the ship was the most important channel of pan-African communication before the invention of the LP record (Gilroy 1995: 13).[1]

Mintz and Price (1976), in their attempt to reveal common traits of social organization in Afro-American and Afro-Caribbean communities, say that the earliest social ties established during the Middle Passage were of a dyadic nature and between people of the same sex. In many parts of Afro-America, the institution of the shipmate relationship became a central point of social organization and remained so for decades and even centuries. In Jamaica the shipmate practically meant brother or sister. It was "the dearest word and bond of affectionate sympathy … and so strong were the bonds between *shipmates* that sexual intercourse between them … was considered incestuous" (Orlando Patterson, quoted by Mintz & Price 1976: 43). It was normal for children to call their parents' shipmates by the terms "uncle" and "aunt." In Surinam the equivalent term—*sippi*—was used between people who had in fact shared the experience of transport aboard the same ship. Later it started being used among slaves who belonged to the same plantation, thus preserving the essential notions of shared suffering. When they wrote their book, Mintz and Price said that among the Saramaka of Surinam, *sippi* (now *sibi*) still designated a special dyadic relationship that was activated when two people were victim of parallel misfortune. The authors also mention other examples: in Trinidad the expression *malongue* designates the same kind of relationship, as do the expressions *máti* in Surinam, *batiment* in Haiti, and *malungo* in Brazil.

Dilazenze Malungo was the name of the character in whose homage the *Bloco Afro* Dilazenze of Ilhéus was named. The dictionary entry could not be more elucidating: "Malungo: (from Kimbundu) 1. Companion, comrade. 2. Name by which Blacks who left Africa on the same ship called each other. 3. (Brazilian) Bosom brother (i.e., fed with the same milk)." What was Dilazenze Malungo's story? Mãe Hilsa explained that he was an African who was her uncle's friend. He was initiated into *Candomblé* with Hilsa's mother. Euzébio Félix Rodrigues plays an important role in the history of Hilza's *terreiro*. He founded his first *terreiro* in Salvador, but he was also the owner of a group of hotels. One day an African called Hipólito Reis took up a room in one of his hotels. According to Mãe Hilsa he was a *babalaô* (*pai-de-santo*) in Africa and was Euzébio's *pai-de-santo*, since Euzébio started his work in *Candomblé* not having been initiated by anyone. Euzébio and Hipólito became great friends and started going to Ilhéus often.

Mãe Hilsa: Hipólito, he came from … South Africa, but I don't know exactly where. He came to Brazil because he was a great friend of my uncle's and became his *pai-de-*

santo. MVA: But they met there … MH: He came … my uncle traveled a lot and in one of his trips to Africa he met that gentleman and invited him to Salvador. He came and did my uncle's *obrigações,*[2] met my mother when she was very young and also initiated her. MVA: He didn't speak Portuguese? MH: No. It was very hard; he spoke very little, if any at all. (From the field diary)

As an African, met aboard a ship, Hipólito Reis or Dilazenze Malungo is seen as the founding hero, someone who places the *terreiro*'s lineage and family in the Africa-Brazil transit. Euzébio, on the other hand, was to found a *terreiro* in Ilhéus in 1915. He ran it until 1941, the year of his death. This was a period of strong economic activity in Ilhéus, centered on cocoa export. It was a port town, a town of sailors and stevedores (the city's first *Bloco Afro* was founded in the stevedores' neighborhood). Besides, all seems to indicate that the flux of Afro-Brazilians into Ilhéus occurred in the first decades of the twentieth century. Migration was by boat, with fixation in port towns and activities. This was also the period of the foundation of the first *terreiro*s in Ilhéus.

Authors who are inclined toward rigid classifications usually distinguish three traditions in Afro-Brazilian religious cults. First there is the more "pure," supposedly more "African" tradition, that of Bahian *Candomblé* of the Nagô "nation." It claims to be the continuation of the Yoruba tradition and is active today in the movements for re-Africanization and antisyncretism. On the other hand, there is a more syncretic *Candomblé,* usually associated with the so-called Angola "nation." Besides African Orixás,[3] entities called *caboclos* also have a place. They are the spirits of Brazilian Indians or people who symbolize certain activities and social characters (slaves, sailors, cowboys, etc.). Finally, there is Umbanda, the religious "synthesis" between African influences and European Kardecist Spiritism. As an urban cult that was promoted as truly Brazilian (i.e., mixed), it gathers all sorts of spiritual entities, especially those that are specifically "made in Brazil." The divisions between the three lines are not as clear in real life. That is why a description of the Sailor in Umbanda could easily apply to *Candomblé* (especially of the Angola nation).

In Umbanda, besides African and Indian spirits, there are also spirits of children, of people who died on other continents, and so on. These spirits are distributed along "lines," each led by an African Orixá and a Catholic saint. Lines are subdivided into "phalanges" or "legions," each led by a non-African and non-Catholic entity: *caboclos* (Brazilian Indians), *pretos velhos* (old Black slaves) and so on. The most common lines are those of *pretos velhos,* Bahians, *boiadeiros* (cowboys), and sailors. A web site on Umbanda provides a bit of the endogenous discourse on the Sailor, describing how the possession of an initiate by a sailor takes place:

Sailor: entity that works in the Line of Waters. Sailors appear in Umbanda stumbling, as if they could not get used to solid ground. Their arms move as if they were rowing…. His colors are blue and white or just white. His guides are shells; his clothes are white or white and blue; his drink is beer and his food is seafood. Sailors: … They come out of their *calunga* ships, with laughter, lots of hugging and hands shaking … Sailors are men and women who sail the seas, who have discovered islands, continents, new worlds. They face both the dead calm and the stormy seas … They work in the line of Iemanjá and Oxum (water people) and bring a message of hope and strength, telling us that we can fight and explore the unknown … Their work is done in *descarregos* [expulsion of bad spirits], *consultas* [answering questions], and *passes*, in the development of mediums and in other jobs that involve sending messages of help. Their work is similar to that of the Exus…[4]

In *Candomblé terreiros* of the "Angola" tradition, like the majority in Ilhéus, the Sailor can appear, too. He is particularly salient in Ilhéus. Jocélio Teles dos Santos (1995) analyzes the figure of the *caboclo* in *Candomblé* as the representation of the "owner of the land," as a "spirit of the place," that is, the symbolic representative of the Indians as the original inhabitants of Brazil, thus reflecting the importance of location and place in African religious thought, whether it is the location of the sacred, of family, or of belonging. The term *caboclo* was semantically expanded to include what in more orthodox milieus would be the *eguns*, or spirits of the ancestors. The Sailor has a special position in this context: he "answers as a *caboclo*," but he is a spirit of the water, not of the land. *Caboclos* are supposed to approach people (Orixás keep a distance and just take hold of the person in trance, without talking), but the Sailor exaggerates that capacity to contact and talk. Telles dos Santos calls the Sailor "a drunken Mercury." His manners also make him resemble the Exu, for he curses, drinks beer and rum, and is an intermediary between people and the spirits. Exu is precisely the entity that is in charge of opening up the ways and roads, and his favorite territory is the crossroads. Edison Carneiro (1986) called the Sailor the "National Mercury."

The sailor is, then, a Mercury (or, if we use the Greek version, a Hermes), a skilled communicator and messenger, talking directly to people in a language they understand. As an archetype, he invokes travels and journeys: those of the maritime expansion and "discoveries," those of the Middle Passage, those of the triangular Atlantic trade between Brazil, Portugal and Africa. Curiously enough, the representations of the Sailor—such as the ceramic dolls sold in *Candomblé* stores in the markets—represent him as a white man. As a matter of fact, the ethnic tag for the Portuguese in Brazil in the years following independence was *marinheiros*.

Now that the five hundred years of Brazil (or of the "discovery" of Brazil, depending on who is talking) were celebrated, could this traveling Sailor—white skin, black mask, in a provocative inversion of Fanon's title—be a symbol of the reformulation (or should I say inversion?) of the images of ships, sailors, and navigations that saturate the Portuguese national(-ist) imagery? Could he be a symbol of other ways of thinking identities and emancipatory movements as more fluid, more transitory? At least he has helped me, ever since a Sailor, embodying a *mãe-de-santo* in trance, told me that I was following a troubled course during fieldwork.

Notes

1. See Linebaugh (1982).
2. *Obrigações* (obligations) are the ritual prescriptions necessary for initiation into *Candomblé*.
3. Orixás are usually defined as African deities that take possession of the initiate during trance in *Candomblé* ritual. They represent royal characters from the beginning of time in the Nigerian cities where the religion originated. They can also be explained as archetypal principles, similar to Roman or Ancient Greek deities. Quotation was extracted from www.nwm.com.br/wgreletronica/orixase.htm.
4. Commonly associated with the Devil, an Exu is rather a Mercury and a trickster. In *Candomblé* one must "send the Exu away" before starting any ceremony. An Exu is a messenger between people and the spirits and Orixás.

BIBLIOGRAPHY

Agier, M. and Carvalho, M. R., 1994, "Nation, Race, Culture: les Mouvements Noirs et Indiens au Brésil," *Cahier des Amériques Latines*, 17.

Ahmad, A., 1995, "The politics of literary postcoloniality," *Race and Class* 36 (3): 1–20.

Alexandre, V., 1979, *Origens do colonialismo português moderno*. Lisbon: Sá da Costa.

Alexandre, V. and Dias, J., eds., 1998, *O Império Africano 1825–1890*, vol. 10, *Nova História da Expansão Portuguesa*, J. Serrão and A. H. Oliveira Marques, eds. Lisbon: Estampa.

Amado, J., 1986, *São Jorge dos Ilhéus*. Lisbon: Europa-América.

Amado, J., 1998, *Gabriela, Cravo e Canela*. Lisbon: Europa-América.

Anderson, B., 1983, *Imagined Communities: Reflections on the Origins and Spread of Nationalism*. London: Verso.

Anderson, B., 1993, "Imagining East Timor," *Arena Magazine*, 4 (April–May); http://www.ci.uc.pt/Timor/imagin.htm.

Appadurai, A., 1986, ed., *The Social Life of Things: Commodities in Cultural Perspective*. Cambridge: Cambridge University Press.

Appadurai, A., 1990, "Disjuncture and Difference in the Global Cultural Economy," *Public Culture* 2 (2): 1–24.

Appiah, K. A., 1997 (1992), *Na Casa de Meu Pai. A África na Filosofia da Cultura*. Rio de Janeiro: Contraponto.

Appiah, K. A., 1997, "Is the 'Post-' in 'Postcolonial' the 'Post-' in 'Postmodern'?" in A. McClintock, et al., eds., 420–444.

Araújo, R. B. de, 1994, *Guerra e Paz. Casa-Grande e Senzala e a Obra de Gilberto Freyre nos Anos 30*. Rio de Janeiro: Editora 34.

Armstrong, J., 1982, *Nations Before Nationalism*. Chapel Hill: University of North Carolina Press.

Asad, T., 1973, *Anthropology and the Colonial Encounter*. London: Ithaca Press.

Ashcroft, B. et al., 1998, *Key Concepts in Postcolonial Studies*. London: Routledge.

Astuti, R., 1995, "'The Vezo are not a kind of people': Identity, difference, and 'ethnicity' among a fishing people of western Madagascar," *American Ethnologist* 22 (3): 464–482.

Azevedo, T. de, 1955, *As Elites de Cor: Um Estudo de Ascensão Social.* São Paulo: Cª Editora Nacional.

Balutansky, K., 1997, "Appreciating C. L. R. James, a Model of Modernity and Creolization," *Latin American Research Review* 32 (2): 233–243.

Barber, K. and Waterman, C., 1995, "Traversing the global and the local: fújì music and praise poetry in the production of contemporary Yorùbá popular culture," in Miller, ed., 1995, 240–262.

Barth, F., ed., 1969, *Ethnic Groups and Boundaries.* Boston: Little, Brown.

Bastide, R., 1958, *Le Candomblé de Bahia, rite Nagô.* Paris: Mouton & Cie.

Bastide, R., 1960/1989, *As Religiões Africanas no Brasil,* 3rd ed. São Paulo: Pioneira.

Bastide, R., 1973, *Estudos Afro-Brasileiros.* São Paulo: Perspectiva.

Bastide, R. and Fernandes, F., 1955, *Relações Raciais entre Negros e Brancos em São Paulo.* São Paulo: UNESCO/Anhembi.

Bastos, C., 1998, "Notas de viagem em Lévi-Strauss e Gilberto Freyre," *Análise Social* 33, 146–147.

Bastos, C., M. Vale de Almeida, B. Feldman-Bianco, eds., 2002, *Trânsitos Coloniais: Diálogos Críticos Luso-Brasileiros,* Lisbon: ICS.

Bhabha, H. K., 1994, *The Location of Culture.* London: Routledge.

Bhabha, H. K., 1997, "The World and the Home", in McClintock et al., eds., 445–455.

Birman, P., 1995, *Fazer Estilo Criando Gêneros. Possessão e diferenças de gênero em terreiros de Umbanda e Candomblé no Rio de Janeiro.* Rio de Janeiro: Relume Dumará/EdUERJ.

Boxer, C., 1963/1988, *Relações raciais no Império colonial português 1415–1825.* Oporto: Afrontamento.

Braga, J., 1995, *Na Gamela do Feitiço: repressão e resistência nos candomblés da Bahia.* Salvador: CEAO/Edufba.

Brereton, B., 1981, *History of Modern Trinidad 1783–1962.* London: Heinemann Educational Books.

Brookshaw, D., 1983, *Raça e Cor na Literatura Brasileira.* Porto Alegre: Mercado Aberto.

Bulmer, M. and Solomos, J., 1998, "Introduction: Re-Thinking Ethnic and Racial Studies," *Ethnic and Racial Studies* 21 (5): 819–837.

Canclini, N. G., 1989/1997, *Culturas Híbridas.* São Paulo: EdUSP.

Carneiro, E., 1935/1988, *Situação do Negro no Brasil. Estudos Afro-Brasileiros.* Recife: Massangana.

Carneiro, E., 1948/1986, *Candomblés da Bahia,* 7th ed. Rio de Janeiro: Civilização Brasileira.

Castells, M., 1997, *The Information Age: Economy, Society and Culture,* 3 vols. Oxford: Blackwell.

Castelo, C., 1998, *O Modo Português de Estar no Mundo. O Luso-Tropicalismo e a Ideologia Colonial Portuguesa (1933–1961).* Oporto: Afrontamento.

Chambers, I. and Curti, L., eds., 1996, *The Postcolonial Question,* London: Routledge.

Chatterjee, P., 1986, *Nationalist Thought and the Colonial World: A Derivative Discourse.* Minneapolis: University of Minnesota Press.

Chatterjee, P., 1993, *The Nation and its fragments: colonial and postcolonial histories.* Princeton: Princeton University Press.

Cinatti, R., 1974/1996, *Paisagens Timorenses com Vultos.* Lisbon: Relógio d'Água.

Clifford, J., 1997, *Routes: Travel and Translation in the Late Twentieth Century.* Cambridge, Mass., and London: Harvard University Press.

Coelho, A., 1890/1993, "Esboço de um Programa para o Estudo Antropológico, Patológico e Demográfico do Povo Português", *Obra Etnográfica,* Vol. 1, *Festas, Costumes e outros Materiais para uma Etnologia de Portugal,* Lisbon: Publicações Dom Quixote, 681–701.

Comaroff, J., 1996, "Ethnicity, Nationalism, and the Politics of Difference in an Age of Revolution," in Wilmsen and McAllister, eds., 162–184.

Cooper, F. and Stoler, A. L., eds., 1997, *Tensions of Empire.* Berkeley: University of California Press.

Corrêa, M., 1996, "Sobre a Invenção da Mulata," *Cadernos Pagu* 6–7: 35–50.

Corrêa, M., 1998, *As Ilusões da Liberdade: a Escola Nina Rodrigues e a Antropologia no Brasil.* Bragança Paulista: EDUSF.

Correia, A. M., 1934, "Os Mestiços nas Colónias Portuguesas," *Comunicação apresentada ao I Congresso Nacional de Antropologia Colonial,* Oporto.

Correia, A. M., 1940, "O Mestiçamento nas Colónias Portuguesas," in *Congresso do Mundo Português,* vol. 14, Tomo 1, Lisbon.

Cortesão, J., 1930/1984, *Os factores democráticos na formação de Portugal.* Lisbon: Horizonte.

Costa e Silva, 1992, *A Enxada e a lança—A África antes dos portugueses.* Rio de Janeiro: Nova Fronteira.

Costa Lima, V., 1977, *A Família de Santo nos Candomblés.* Salvador: UFBa.

Costa Pinto, A., 1999, "A Guerra Colonial e o Fim do Império Português," in F. Bethencourt and K. Chaudhuri, eds., *História da Expansão Portuguesa,* vol. 5. Lisbon: Círculo de Leitores, 65–101.

Crockford, F., 2000, "Reconciling Worlds: The Cultural Repositioning of East Timorese Youth in the Diaspora," in J. Fox and D: B. Soares, eds., *Out of the Ashes: Destruction and Reconstruction of East Timor.* Adelaide: Crawford Publishing House, 223–234.

Cunha, M. C. da, 1986, *Antropologia do Brasil: mito, história, etnicidade.* São Paulo: Brasiliense.

DaMatta, R., 1981, "Você sabe com quem está falando?" in *Carnaváis, Malandros e Heróis,* 3rd Ed. Rio de Janeiro: Zahar.

DaMatta, R., 1987, "Digressão: A Fábula das Três Raças ou o Problema do Racismo à Brasileira," in *Relativizando: Uma Introdução à Antropologia Social.* Rio de Janeiro: Rocco.

Dantas, B. G., 1982, "Repensando a pureza Nagô", *Religião e Sociedade* 8: 15–20.

Dantas, B. G., 1989, *Vovô Nagô e Papai Branco. Usos e Abusos da África no Brasil.* Rio de Janeiro: Graal.

Dantas, M., 1996, "Gestão, cultura e leadership. O caso de três organizações Afro-baianas" in T. Fischer, ed., *Gestão Contemporânea. Cidades Estratégicas e Organizações Locais.* Rio de Janeiro: Editora da Fundação Getúlio Vargas, 151–163.

D'Aquino, I., 1983, *Capoeira: Strategies for Status, Power and Identity,* Ph. D. Dissertation in anthropology, University of Illinois.

Degler, C., 1971/1986, *Neither Black nor White: Slavery and Race Relations in Brazil and the United States.* Madison: University of Wisconsin Press.

Dias, J., 1950/1990, "Os elementos fundamentais da cultura portuguesa", *Estudos de Antropologia*, vol. 1. Lisbon: INCM.

Dias, J., 1956/1990, "Paralelismo de processo na formação das nações," in *Estudos de Antropologia*, vol. 1, Lisbon: INCM.

Dias, J., 1971, "Estudos do carácter nacional português," *Estudos de Antropologia Cultural*, 7. Lisbon: Junta de Investigações do Ultramar.

Dirlik, A., 1994, *After the Revolution: Waking to Global Capitalism*. Hanover, N. H.: University Press of New England.

Dirlik, A., 1997, "The postcolonial aura: Third world criticism in the age of global capitalism," in McClintock et al., eds., 501–528.

Fanon, F., n.d. (1952), *Peau Noire, Masques Blancs*. Paris: Seuil.

Ferguson, C. A., 1985, "Diglossia", in P. P. Giglioli, ed., *Language and Social Context*, Harmondsworth: Penguin, 232–251.

Fernandes, F., 1965/1985, *A Integração do Negro na Sociedade de Classes*. São Paulo: Ática.

Ferreira, J.-A., 1994, *The Portuguese of Trinidad and Tobago. Portrait of an Ethnic Minority*. St. Augustine: Institute of Social and Economic Research, The University of the West Indies.

Ferreira, M., n.d., *A Aventura Crioula*, 3rd ed. Lisbon: Plátano.

Fontaine, P. M., ed., 1985, *Race, Class and Power in Brazil*. Los Angeles: Center for Afro-American Studies, University of California.

Fradique, T., 1998, *"Culture is in the house": O Rap em Portugal, a Retórica da Tolerância e as Políticas de Definição de Produtos Culturais*, Dissertação de Mestrado em Antropologia, ISCTE, Lisbon.

Freitas Branco, J., 1986, *Camponeses da Madeira: As bases materiais do quotidiano no arquipélago (1750–1900)*. Lisbon: Dom Quixote.

Freyre, G., 1933/1992, *Casa-Grande e Senzala. Formação da família brasileira sob o regime da economia patriarcal* (Vol. I of *Introdução à história da sociedade patriarcal no Brasil*), 29th ed. Rio de Janeiro: Record.

Freyre, G., 1940/1955, "Uma cultura ameaçada: a luso-brasileira," in *Um Brasileiro em terras Portuguesas*.

Freyre, G., 1951, *O mundo que o português criou. Aspectos das relações sociais e de cultura do Brasil com Portugal e as colónias portuguesas*. Preface by António Sérgio. Lisbon: Livros do Brasil.

Freyre, G., 1955, *Um Brasileiro em Terras Portuguesas. Introdução a uma possível luso-tropicologia, acompanhada de conferências e discursos proferidos em Portugal e em terras lusitanas e ex-lusitanas da Ásia, da África e do Atlântico*. Lisbon: Livros do Brasil.

Freyre, G., 1958, "Integração Portuguesa nos Trópicos. Notas em torno de uma possível lusotropicologia que se especializasse no estudo sistemático do processo ecológico-social de integração de portugueses, descendentes de portugueses e continuadores de portugueses, em ambientes tropicais," *Estudos de Ciências Políticas e Sociais*, 1 ("Política Ultramarina"). Lisbon: Junta de Investigações do Ultramar.

Freyre, G., 1961, *O Luso e o Trópico. Sugestões em torno dos métodos portugueses de integração de povos autóctones e de culturas diferentes da europeia num complexo novo de civilização: o luso-tropical*. Lisbon: Comissão executiva das comemorações do V centenário da morte do Infante Dom Henrique (Congresso Internacional de História dos Descobrimentos).

Freyre, G., 1963, *O Brasil em face das Áfricas Negras e Mestiças*. Lisbon: Edição de um grupo de amigos e admiradores portugueses para distribuir gratuitamente às escolas.

Fry, P., 1995–96, "O que a Cinderela Negra Tem a Dizer sobre a 'Política Racial' no Brasil," *Revista USP*, 28 (Dossier Povo Negro—300 Anos).

Geertz, C., 1980/1991, *Negara. O Estado Teatro no Século XIX*. Lisbon: Difel.

Gellner, E., 1973, "Scale and Nation," *Philosophy of the Social Sciences* 3: 1–17.

Gellner, E., 1983, *Nations and Nationalism*. Oxford: Blackwell.

Giddens, A., 1994, "Living in a post traditional society," in S. Lash, ed., *Reflexive Modernization: Politics, Tradition and Aesthetics in the Modern Social Order*. Cambridge: Polity.

Gilliam, A., 1997, "Globalização, Identidade e os Ataques à Igualdade nos Estados Unidos," *Revista Crítica de Ciências Sociais*, 48: 67–101.

Gilroy, P., 1987, *There Ain't no Black in the Union Jack*. London: Routledge.

Gilroy, P., 1993/1995, *The Black Atlantic. Modernity and Double Consciousness*. London: Verso.

Gilroy, P., 1996, "Route Work: The Black Atlantic and the politics of exile," in Chambers and Curti, eds., 17–29.

Godinho, V. M., 1964/1984, "Prefácio" to J. Cortesão, 1930/1984, *Os factores democráticos na formação de Portugal*. Lisbon: Horizonte.

Goldman, M., 1985, "A Construção Ritual da Pessoa: A Possessão no Candomblé," *Religião e Sociedade* 12 (1): 22–53.

Goldman, M., 2000, "Uma teoria etnográfica da democracia. A política do ponto de vista do movimento negro de Ilhéus, Bahia, Brasil," *Etnográfica*, 2 (4): 311–332.

Gomes, A. M., 1978, *All Papa's Children*. Surrey: Cairi Publishing House.

Guimarães, A. S., 1995, "Racismo e anti-racismo no Brasil," *Novos-Estudos-CEBRAP* 43: 26–44.

Habermas, J., 1987, *The Philosophical Discourse of Modernity*. Cambridge, Mass.: MIT Press.

Hall, S., 1992/1997, *Identidades culturais na pós-modernidade*. Rio de Janeiro: DP&A Editora.

Hall, S., 1996, "When was 'the postcolonial'? Thinking at the limit," in Chambers and Curti, eds., 242–260.

Hanchard, M. G., 1994, *Orpheus and Power: The "Movimento Negro" of Rio de Janeiro and São Paulo, Brazil, 1945–1988*. Princeton: Princeton University Press.

Hanchard, M., 1997, "Americanism and Brazilianism," 20th International Congress of the Latin American Studies Association, Guadalajara, Mexico, 17–19 April.

Handler, R., 1984, "On Sociocultural Discontinuity: Nationalism and Cultural Objectification in Quebec," *Current Anthropology* 25 (1): 55–71.

Handler, R., 1988, *Nationalism and the Politics of Culture in Quebec*. Madison: University of WisconsinPress.

Hannerz, U., 1992, *Cultural Complexity: Studies in the Social Organization of Meaning*. New York: Columbia University Press.

Haraway, D., 1989, *Primate Visions: Gender, Race and Nature in the World of Modern Science*. New York: Routledge.

Haraway, D., 1991, *Simians, Cyborgs and Women—the Reinvention of Nature*. New York: Routledge.

Harris, M., 1964, *Patterns of Race in the Americas*. New York: Crowell.

Harris, M., 1970, "Referential Ambiguity in the Calculus of Brazilian Racial Identity,"*Southwestern Journal of Anthropology* 26: 1–14.

Hasenbalg, C., 1979, *Discriminação e Desigualdades Raciais no Brasil*. Rio de Janeiro: Graal.

Hasenbalg, C., 1985, "Race and Socioeconomic Inequalities in Brazil," in P. M.Fontaine, ed., *Race, Class and Power in Brazil*. Los Angeles: Center for Afro-American Studies, University of California.

Hasenbalg, C., 1995, "Entre o Mito e os Fatos: Racismo e Relações Raciais no Brasil," *Dados*, 38 (2): 355–374.

Hasenbalg, C. and Valle e Silva, N., 1988, *Estrutura Social, Mobilidade e Raça*. São Paulo: Vértice e IUPERJ.

Hasenbalg, C. and Valle e Silva, N.,1993a, "Notas Sobre Desigualdade Racial e Política no Brasil," *Estudos Afro-Asiáticos*, 25: 141–160.

Hasenbalg, C. and Valle e Silva, N., 1993b, *Relações Raciais no Brasil Contemporâneo*. Rio de Janeiro: Rio Fundo Editora.

Hayden, R., 1996, "Imagined Communities and Real Victims: Self-Determination and Ethnic Cleansing in Yugoslavia," *American Ethnologist* 23 (4): 783–801.

Herskovits, M. J., 1943, "The Negro in Bahia, Brazil: a problem in method," *American Sociological Review*, 7.

Hobsbawm, E., 1996, "Identity Politics and the Left," *New Left Review* 217: 38–47.

Holanda, S. B., 1936/1996, *Raízes do Brasil*. São Paulo: Companhia das Letras.

Hutchinson, H., 1952, "Race Relations in a Rural Community of Bahia Recôncavo," in H. Hutchinson, ed.,*Race and Class in Rural Brasil*. Paris: UNESCO.

Ianni, O., 1962, *As Metamorfoses do Escravo*. São Paulo: Difel.

Jackson, M., ed., 1996, *Things As They Are. New Directions in Phenomenological Anthropology*. Bloomington: Indiana University Press.

Jameson, F., 1984, "Postmodernism or the Cultural Logic of Late Capitalism," *New Left Review* 146: 53–92.

Kahn, J. S., 1995, *Culture, Multiculture, Postculture*. London: Sage.

Khan, A., 1993, "What is a 'Spanish'? Ambiguity and 'mixed' ethnicity in Trinidad," in Yelvington, ed., 180–207.

Kopytoff, I., 1986, "The Cultural Biography of Things: Commoditization as Process," in Appadurai, ed., 64–91.

Landes, R., 1947/1967, *A Cidade das Mulheres*. Rio de Janeiro: Civilização Brasileira.

Latour, B., 1991/1994, *Jamais Fomos Modernos*. Rio de Janeiro: Editora 34.

Leal, J., 2000a, "Psicologia Étnica: Invenção e Circulação de Estereóptios," ch. 3 of *Etnografias Portuguesas (1870–1970) Cultura Popular e Identidade Nacional*, Lisbon, Dom Quixote, 83–104.

Leal, J., 2000b, "A Sombra Esquiva dos Lusitanos: Exercícios de Etnogenealogia," ch. 2 of *Etnografias Portuguesas (1870–1970) Cultura Popular e Identidade Nacional*, Lisbon, Dom Quixote, 63–82.

Leite, I. B., ed., 1996, *Negros no Sul do Brasil: invisibilidade e territorialidade*. Florianópolis: Letras Contemporâneas.

Lima, J. A. Pires de, 1940, "Influência dos Mouros, Judeus e Negros na Etnografia Portuguesa," in *Congresso do Mundo Português*, vol. 28, Lisbon.

Linebaugh, P., 1982, "All the Atlantic Mountains Shook", *Labour/Le Travailleur*, 10: 87–121.

Linnekin, J. and Poyer, L. 1990. "Introduction" and "The Politics of Culture in the Pacific," in J. Linnekin and L. Poyer, *Cultural Identity and Ethnicity in the Pacific*. Honolulu: University of Hawaii Press, 4–16.

Lourenço, E., 1978/1982, "Psicanálise mítica do destino português" in Lourenço 1982.

Lourenço, E., 1982, *O labirinto da saudade. Psicanálise mítica do destino português*, 2nd ed. Lisbon: Dom Quixote.

Lusotopie, 1997, vol. on *Lusotropicalismo. Idéologies coloniales et identités nationales dans les mondes lusophones*. Paris: Karthala.

Lutz, N. M., 1995, "Colonization, Decolonization and Integration: Language Policies in East Timor, Indonesia." http://www.ci.uc.pt/Timor/language.htm.

Maggie, Y., 1975, *Guerra de Orixá: um estudo de ritual e conflito*. Rio de Janeiro: Zahar.

Maggie, Y., 1993, "Florestan Fernandes e as Categorias Nativas," in *Encontros com a Antropologia*, 73–83. Curitiba: Universidade Federal do Paraná.

Maio, M. C. and Santos, R. V., eds., 1996/1998, *Raça, Ciência e Sociedade*. Rio de Janeiro: Fiocruz.

Marotti, G., 1975, *Perfil Sociológico da Literatura Brasileira*. Oporto: Paisagem.

Marx, A. W., 1996, "A construção da raça e o estado-nação," *Estudos Afro-Asiáticos*, 29.

McClintock, A., 1992, "The Angel of Progress: Pitfalls of the Term Postcolonialism," *Social Text* 31/32: 84–98.

McClintock, A., 1995, *Imperial Leather*. London: Routledge.

McClintock, A. et al., eds., 1997, *Dangerous Liaison:. Gender, Nation, and Postcolonial Perspectives*. Minneapolis: University of Minnesota Press.

Melo, E. Cabral de, 1996, "Posfácio" a Sérgio Buarque de Holanda, *Raízes do Brasil*. São Paulo: Companhia das Letras.

Miller, D., 1994, *Modernity, an Ethnographic Approach. Dualism and Mass Consumption in Trinidad*. Oxford: Berg.

Miller, D., ed., 1995, *Worlds Apart. Modernity through the Prism of the Local*. London: Routledge.

Mintz, S. and Price, R., 1976, *An Anthropological Approach to the Study of Afro-American History: A Caribbean Perspective*. Philadelphia: ISHI.

Moreira, A., 1957, "Política Ultramarina," *Estudos de Ciências Políticas e Sociais*, 1. Lisbon: Junta de Investigações do Ultramar.

Moreira, A., 1958/1963, "Contribuição de Portugal para a valorização do homem no Ultramar," *Ensaios*, 3rd ed., *Estudos de Ciências Políticas e Sociais*, 34. Lisbon: Junta de Investigações do Ultramar.

Moreira, A., 1960, "Problemas Sociais do Ultramar," *Ensaios, Estudos de Ciências Políticas e Sociais*, 34.

Moreira, A., 1961, "Política de integração," *Discurso proferido pelo Ministro do Ultramar na Associação Comercial do Porto*. Lisbon.

Moreira, A., 1963, *Ensaios*, 3rd ed., *Estudos de Ciências Políticas e Sociais*, 34. Lisbon: Junta de Investigações do Ultramar.

Naipaul, V.S., 1962, *The Middle Passage. Impressions of Five Societies—British, French and Dutch—in the West Indies and South America*. Harmondsworth: Penguin.

Naipaul, V.S., 1967/1985, *The Mimic Men*. New York: Vintage.

Nogueira, O., 1955, "Preconceito Racial de Marca e Preconceito Racial de Origem," in *Anais do XXXI Congresso Internacional de Americanistas*, vol. 1. São Paulo.

Norvell, J., 1997, "Feito na Cama: Race Mixture and Genealogies of Brazilian Civilizations," 20th Congresso Internacional da L.A.S.A., Guadalajara, Mexico, 17–19 April.

O'Hanlon, R. and Washbrook, D., 1992, "After Orientalism: Culture, criticism and politics in the third world," *Comparative Studies in Society and History*, 34 (1).

Oliveira, C., 1996, *Portugal. Dos Quatro Cantos do Mundo à Descolonização, 1974–1976*. Lisbon: Cosmos.

Omi, M. and Winant, H., 1986, *Racial Formation in the United States*. New York: Routledge.

Ong, A., 1996, "Anthropology, China and Modernities: The geopolitics of cultural knowledge" in H. Moore, ed., *The future of Anthropological Knowledge*. London: Routledge.

Ortiz, R., 1978, *A Morte Branca do Feiticeiro Negro*. São Paulo: Brasiliense.

Pereira, R., 1986, "Antropologia aplicada na política colonial portuguesa do Estado Novo," *Revista Internacional de Estudos Africanos* 4–5: 191–235.

Pierson, D., 1942/1967, *Negroes in Brazil: A Study of Race Contact in Bahia*. Carbondale: Southern Illinois University Press.

Pimentel, I., 1998, "O Aperfeiçoamento da Raça. A Eugenia na Primeira Metade do Século XX," *História*, no. 3, ano 20, nova série, 18–27.

Pina-Cabral, J., 1998, "Racismo ou etnocentrismo?", in H. G. Araújo, ed., *Nós e os Outros: A Exclusão em Portugal e na Europa*, 19–26. Oporto: SPAE.

Prakash, G., 1990, "Writing post-orientalist histories of the third world: perspectives from Indian historiography," *Comparative Studies inSociety and History*, 32 (3): 383–408

Prakash, G., 1997, "Postcolonial criticism and Indian historiography," in McClintock et al., eds.,491–500.

Prandi, R., 1991, *Os Candomblés de São Paulo*. São Paulo: Hucitec/EdUSP.

Queiroz Jr., T., 1975, *Preconceito de Cor e a Mulata na Literatura Brasileira*. São Paulo: Ática.

Reis, C., 1945, *Associação Portuguesa Primeiro de Dezembro*. Port-of-Spain: Yuille's Printery.

Reis, J. J., ed., 1988, *Escravidão e Invenção da Liberdade: Estudos sobre o Negro no Brasil*. Editora Brasiliense/CNPq.

Reis, J. J. and Silva, E., 1989, *Negociação e Conflito: A Resistência Negra no Brasil Escravista*. São Paulo: Companhia das Letras.

Reis, L. V. de S., 1997, *O mundo de pernas para o ar. A capoeira no Brasil*. São Paulo: Publisher Brasil.

Ribard, F., 1999, *Le Carnaval Noir de Bahia. Ethnicité, identité, fête Afro a Salvador*. Paris: L'Harmattan.

Robotham, D., 1997, "Postcolonialités: le défi des nouvelles modernités," *RevueInternationalle des SciencesSociales*, 153: 393–408.

Saïd, E., 1978, *Orientalism*. New York: Pantheon.

Saïd, E., 1983, *The World, the Text and the Critic*. Cambridge, Mass.: Harvard University Press.

Sanches, M. R., 1999, "Nas margens: os estudos culturais e o assalto às fronteiras académicas e disciplinares," *Etnográfica* 3 (1): 193–210.

Sansone, L., 1996, "As Relações Raciais em Casa Grande e Senzala Revisitadas à Luz do Processo de Internacionalização e Globalização," in Maio and Santos, eds., 207–218.

Sansone, L. and Santos, J. T., orgs., 1998, *Ritmos em Trânsito. Sócio-antropologia da Música Baiana*. Salvador: Dynamis editorial.

Santos, B. Sousa, 1994a, "Modernidade, identidade e a cultura de fronteira," in *Pela Mão de Alice* ... , 119–140.

Santos, B. Sousa, 1994b, "Onze teses por ocasião de mais uma descoberta de Portugal," in *Pela Mão de Alice* ... , 49–68.

Santos, B. Sousa, 1994c, *Pela mão de Alice. O social e o político na pós-modernidade*. Oporto: Afrontamento.

Santos, G. D., 1996, *Topografias Imaginárias: As Estórias de Eusébio Tamagnini no Instituto de Antropologia de Coimbra, 1902–1952*, Trabalho final de Licenciatura, Deptº de Antropologia, Universidade de Coimbra. Unpublished manuscript.

Santos, J. T., 1995, *O dono da terra: o caboclo nos candomblés da Bahia*. Salvador: Sarah Letras.

Schiller, N. G. and Fouron, G., 1997, "'Laços de Sangue': Os Fundamentos Raciais do Estado-Nação Transnacional," *Revista Crítica de Ciências Sociais* 48: 33–61.

Schwarcz, L. M., 1993, *O Espectáculo das Raças: Cientistas, Instituições e Questão Racial no Brasil 1870–1930*. São Paulo: Companhia das Letras.

Scott, D., 1992, "Theory and postcolonial claims on anthropological disciplinarity," *Critique of Anthropology* 12 (4): 371–394.

Scott, D., 1996, "Postcolonial criticism and the claims of political modernity," *Social Text* 48 (3): 1–26.

Scott, J., 1985, *Weapons of the Weak: Everyday Forms of Peasant Resistance*. New Haven: Yale University Press.

Segal, D. and Handler, R., 1995, "U.S. Multiculturalism and the Concept of Culture," *Identities* 1 (4): 391–407.

Sérgio, António, 1951, "Prefácio", in Freyre, G., *O mundo que o português criou. Aspectos das relações sociais e de cultura do Brasil com Portugal e as colónias portuguesas*. Lisbon: Livros do Brasil.

Seyferth, G., 1991, "Os Paradoxos da Miscigenação: Observações sobre o Tema Imigração e Raça no Brasil," *Estudos Afro-Asiáticos* 20: 165–185.

Seyferth, G., 1996/1998, "Construindo a Nação: Hierarquias Raciais e o Papel do Racismo na Política de Imigração e Colonização," in Maio and Santos, eds., 41–58.

Shohat, E., 1992, "Notes on the 'Postcolonial'", *Social Text* 31/32: 99–103.

Silva, A. C. C., 1998, *A Cidadania no Ritmo do Movimento Black de Ilhéus*, Dissertação de Mestrado em Antropologia Social, Universidade Federal do Rio de Janeiro.

Silverman, S., 1976, "Ethnicity as Adaptation: Strategies and Systems," *Reviews in Anthropology* 3: 626–636.

Siqueira, M. L., 1996, "Ancestralidade e contemporaneidade de organizações de resistência Afro-brasileira," in T. Fischer, ed., *Gestão Contemporânea. Cidades Estratégicas e Organizações Locais*. Rio de Janeiro: Editora da Fundação Getúlio Vargas, 133–149.

Skidmore, T. E. 1989. *Preto no Branco: Raça e Nacionalidade no Pensamento Brasileiro.* Rio de Janeiro: Paz e Terra.

Skidmore, T. E., 1994, *O Brasil Visto de Fora.* São Paulo: Paz e Terra.

Smith, A. D., 1994, "The Politics of Culture: Ethnicity and Nationalism," in T. Ingold, ed., *Companion Encyclopaedia of Anthropology.* London: Routledge.

Smith, L. S., Jr., ed., 1950, *Trinidad—Who, What, Why.*Port-of-Spain: L. S. Smith.

Spivak, G. C., 1990, *The Post-colonial Critic: Interviews, Strategies, Dialogues.* New York: Routledge.

Stepan, N., 1986, "Race and Gender: The Role of Analogy in Science," in S. Harding, ed., 1986/1993, *The Racial Economy of Science,* Bloomington and Indianapolis: Indiana University Press.

Stolcke, V., 1995, "Talking culture: new boundaries, new rhetorics of exclusion in Europe," *Current Anthropology* 36 (1): 1–13.

Stoler, A. L., 1997, "Making Empire Respectable: The Politics of Race and Sexual Morality in Twentieth-Century Colonial Cultures," in McClintock, A. et al., eds., 344–373.

Strathern, M., 1988, *The Gender of the Gift.* Berkeley: University of California Press.

Tavares, J. C. de S., 1984, "Dança da guerra: arquivo-arma," dissertação de Mestrado, Sociologia, Universidade de Brasília.

Turner, Victor, 1969, *The Ritual Process. Structure and Anti-Structure.* Ithaca: Cornell University Press.

Turner, T., 1991, "Representing, Resisting, Rethinking: Historical Transformations of Kayapo Culture and Anthropological Consciousness," in G. W. Stocking, ed., *Colonial Situations: Essays on the Contextualization of Ethnographic Knowledge.* Madison: University of Wisconsin Press, 285–313.

Vala, J. et al., 1999, *Expressões dos Racismos em Portugal.* Lisbon: ICS.

Vale de Almeida, M., 1996, *The Hegemonic Male. Masculinity in a Portuguese Town.* Oxford and New York: Berghahn Books.

Vale de Almeida, M., 2000, *Um Mar da Cor da Terra. "Raça", Cultura e Política da Identidade.* Oeiras (Portugal): Celta.

Valverde, P., 1997, "O corpo e a busca de lugares de perfeição: escritas missionárias da África colonial portuguesa, 1930–60", *Etnográfica* 1 (1): 73–96.

Vasconcelos, J., 1997, "Tempos Remotos: A Presença do Passado na Objectificação da Cultura Local," *Etnográfica* 1 (2): 213–236.

Venâncio, J. C., 1996, *Colonialismo, antropologia e lusofonias: repensando a presença portuguesa nos trópicos.* Lisbon: Vega.

Vertovec, S., 1996, "Multiculturalism, Culturalism and Public Incorporation," *Ethnic and Racial Studies* 19 (1): 49–69.

Viegas, S. M., 1998, "Índios que Não Querem Ser Índios: Etnografia Localizada e Identidades Multi-Referenciais," *Etnográfica* 2 (1): 91–112.

Wade, P., n.d., "Race, nature and culture," *Man*, NS, 28: 17–34.

Wade, P., 1993, *Blackness and Race Mixture. The Dynamics of Racial Identity in Colombia.* Baltimore and London: The Johns Hopkins Press.

Wade, P., 1997, *Race and Ethnicity in Latin America.* London: Pluto Press.

Wagley, C., 1951, *Race and Class in Rural Brazil.* Paris: UNESCO.

Weatherbee, D. E., 1966, "Portuguese Timor: An Indonesian Dilemma," *Asian Survey*, 6 (December).

Werbner, R. and Ranger, T., eds., 1996, *Postcolonial Identities in Africa.* London: Zed Books.

Williams, B., 1991, *Stains on My Name, War in My Veins: Guyana and the Politics of Cultural Struggle.* Durham: Duke University Press.

Wilmsen, E. and McAllister, P., eds., 1996, *The Politics of Difference: Ethnic Premises in a World of Power.* Chicago: University of Chicago Press.

Wolf, E., 1982, *Europe and the People Without History.* Berkeley: University of California Press.

Yanagisako, S. and Delaney, C., eds., 1995, *Naturalizing Power: Essays in Feminist Cultural Analysis.* New York: Routledge.

Yelvington, K., ed., 1993, *Trinidad Ethnicity.* London: Macmillan.

Young, R., 1995, *Colonial Desire. Hybridity in Theory, Culture and Race.* London: Routledge.

INDEX